2nd Edition

100

THINGS TO DO IN

CLEVELAND
BEFORE YOU
DIE

D0684428

100
2nd Edition

THINGS TO DO IN
CLEVELAND
BEFORE YOU
DIE

• •

DEB THOMPSON AND TONYA PRATER

REEDY PRESS

Library of Congress Control Number: 2018945635

ISBN: 9781681061672

Design by Jill Halpin

Cover photo: Courtesy of Ilene Safron

Printed in the United States of America
18 19 20 21 22   5 4 3 2 1

Please note that websites, phone numbers, addresses, and company names are subject to change or cancellation. We did our best to relay the most accurate information available, but due to circumstances beyond our control, please do not hold us liable for misinformation. When exploring new destinations, please do your homework before you go.

DEDICATION

To all the travelers and adventure seekers, whether by foot or by armchair. May your quest for discovering new and wonderful corners of this world never end.

• •

CONTENTS

● ●

Music and Entertainment

● ●

• •

Culture and History

• •

Shopping and Fashion

• •

PREFACE

In a city that is ever changing, it feels almost offensive to share only one hundred things to do because Cleveland has much more to offer. Cleveland is full of movers and shakers, artists and musicians, and a melting pot of cultures from around the world. It is a place where you can shop the stalls at a night market in AsiaTown or listen to happy polka tunes. The city is as diverse as the people who call it home.

It's a city that has seen many changes over the years. Located in the Rust Belt, you'll find that its tough and gritty exterior is a cover for the endless wonders you'll discover as you read through the pages of this book.

Cleveland is immersed in music, both new and old. You can indulge in the musical history of this great country at the Rock & Roll Hall of Fame and then go down the road to watch freshly pressed vinyl transformed into a musical masterpiece or attend any number of music-centric events.

Beyond its musical roots, you'll find a great number of outdoor and nature activities that can be surprising for what many may consider a cement jungle. Kayak one of the many rivers, stroll through different continents at Metroparks Zoo, or strap on your skis for some downhill winter fun.

Limiting the book to one hundred things was a challenge. As you begin to explore, you'll uncover one hundred more, and you'll discover why so many people love calling Cleveland home.

We wrote this book to share what we love most about this city that is always evolving and constantly improving. Our hope is that by the time you turn the last page and have explored the city through our eyes, you'll wonder what took you so long to discover this hidden Midwest gem.

FOOD AND DRINK

GET IT STACKED HIGH
AT SLYMAN'S DELI

As you'll quickly discover, Cleveland has a lot of great food, but if you only have time to try one thing, you're going to want to stand in line for a Slyman's corned beef sandwich. Located in a small, nondescript brick building at the corner of St. Clair Avenue and Thirty-First Street, Slyman's has been piling up five inches of thinly sliced, juicy cuts of corned beef on soft rye bread for the past fifty years. The price of the sandwich may come as a surprise, but once your plate arrives and you take that first delightful bite, you'll understand why customers don't mind standing in long lines to get their hands on this Cleveland tradition. Don't be late. Slyman's closes after lunch.

3106 St. Clair Ave. NE
216-621-3760
slymans.com

TASTE THE WORLD
AT THE WEST SIDE MARKET

Be swept away in a cacophony of scents and sounds as you step inside the West Side Market, Cleveland's oldest operating municipally owned market. The food vendors represent the diverse cultural makeup of the Greater Cleveland area, offering cannolis, potato pancakes, bratwurst, empanadas, pierogies, and many more delightful treats. Before grabbing your favorite foods to satisfy your lunchtime hunger, walk upstairs to the balcony to get a bird's-eye view of the hustle and bustle on the floor and a closer look at the Guastavino tile ceilings. Those who are hungry for more than food will be tempted by the historical features of this 1912 building, including the 137-foot clock tower that greets customers at the front entrance. The West Side Market is a feast for your eyes and your stomach!

1979 W. Twenty-Fifth St., Ohio City
216-664-3387
westsidemarket.org

WANT CHUNKY PEANUT BUTTER ON YOUR HOT DOG?
YEP, HAPPY DOG CAN DO THAT

Take a friendly neighborhood bar up a few notches and you have the Happy Dog, an iconic Cleveland bar, located in the must-visit Gordon Square Arts District. People come for the unique hot dogs (veggie, vegan, and gluten free available) and stay for the great music. Belly up to the original oval-shaped bar and order a locally made gourmet hot dog that can be topped with fifty different toppings.

Chunky peanut butter? No problem. Froot Loops? You bet. Bacon-spiked Southern-fried cabbage? They've got that. All three together? If you insist . . . and don't forget to throw down on a side of tots with thirty topping choices.

Stick around after your eclectic meal and enjoy live music—from DJs spinning tunes to a polka band and everything in between, happening nearly every night.

5801 Detroit Ave.
216-651-9474
happydogcleveland.com

TIP

A visit to the Gordon Square Arts
District isn't complete without a stop at the
Superelectric Parlor, located located one block
away. Twenty different pinball machines are
waiting for you to show off your mad skills.

6500 Detroit Ave.
419-215-8797
superelectric.tv

FIND YOUR EATS
ON FOURTH STREET

Hanging lights dangle above the brick-lined street, bringing a fun, party atmosphere to the crowds milling about on Fourth Street. Locals and visitors alike enjoy the ambiance of this hidden foodie and fun treasure in the heart of Cleveland. Some of the best chefs in the nation have discovered that Clevelanders love good food and have opened restaurants in the happening Fourth Street destination. Enjoy bites from Michael Symon's Lola or head over to Pickwick and Frolic to indulge in Ohio's only champagne bar. More than ten restaurants serve fantastic food along this stretch, the Greenhouse Tavern, from James Beard Award-winning chef Jonathon Sawyer. Besides being a food lover's mecca, Fourth Street offers entertainment, from bowling to a comedy club, with a bit of shopping thrown in the mix just for fun.

2015 E. Fourth St.
216-589-1111
east4thstreet.com

TIP
Complete your visit to Fourth Street by taking a ride around downtown on a pedicab. These athletic peddlars from Ride On Cleveland are the best tour guides in the city and in the know about what is hot in the CLE.

PREPARE TO GET MESSY
WITH THE POLISH BOY

It's unlike anything else—a marriage of kielbasa, French fries, coleslaw, and Barbeque sauce. This messy creation is available around town, and a few joints even offer their own unique rendition of the Polish Boy.

Al & B's Barbecue offers the traditional Polish Boy, topping it off with their famous BBQ sauce.

Head over to Hot Sauce Williams to try their verison topped with their special sauce. Best known for their appearance on Man v. Food in which the Polish Girl (like the Polish Boy but add a helping of pulled pork on top) was featured.

Banter Beer and Wine in the Gordon Square Arts District is another not-to-miss Polish Boy establishment. Besides its famous Polish Boy, it has a delicious assortment of poutine.

Al & B's Barbecue
15115 Puritas Ave.
216-362-8601

Hot Sauce Williams
3770 Lee Rd.   12310 Superior Ave.
216-921-4704   216-851-7788

Banter Beer and Wine
7320 Detroit Ave.
216-801-0305
bantercleveland.com

TAKE IT TO THE FLATS

From family-friendly to adults-only parties, Cleveland Flats features a lifestyle uniquely its own. This is the place to dine and play in the city. During the day, take the children and enjoy lunch at Margaritaville or Backyard Bocce while playing a couple of games. At night, plan to eat well and party harder. Start at Magnolia for a pre-dinner craft cocktail or Thirsty Dog Brewing for a pint or two from their forty-plus tap handles. After starting the night with a cocktail, step over to Alley Cat Oyster Bar for dinner with magnificent river views. Wind up the night at the Big Bang Dueling Pianos bar or FWD, where they take nightlife to a whole new level.

Margaritaville
1150 Front Ave., Cleveland Flats
216-615-8855
margaritavillecleveland.com

Backyard Bocce
1059 Old River Rd., Ste. 2, Cleveland Flats
216-523-1507
backyardbocceflats.com

Magnolia
1167 Front Ave., Cleveland Flats
216-990-2300
magnoliacleveland.com

Alley Cat Oyster Bar
1056 Old River Rd., Cleveland Flats
216-574-9999
alleycatoysterbar.com

Thirsty Dog Brewing
1075 Old River Rd., Ste. 2, Cleveland Flats
216-523-1501
thirstydogeastbank.com

Big Bang Dueling Pianos
1163 Front Ave., Cleveland Flats
216-417-6222
thebigbangbar.com

FWD
1176 Front Ave., Cleveland Flats
fwdnightclub.com

DOUBLE DIP YOUR ICE CREAM—IT'S OK!

Nothing screams summer like a big double dip ice cream cone. Fortunately, you don't have to go far to find a cool, refreshing ice cream treat. Honey Hut Ice Cream is a long-standing favorite for Clevelanders and now has five stands across the Greater Cleveland area. Cooper's Twist & Shake has been serving up old-fashioned sundaes for more than fifty years. In Ohio City, Mitchell's Homemade is scooping up handcrafted ice cream that they make in small batches. Watch the magic happen from one of the kitchen viewing windows, or for a special treat, take a tasting tour. At Zero Below in Cleveland Heights, select an ice cream roll, a Thai specialty, instead of a scoop.

TIP

While in Ohio City, be sure to stroll along Twenty-Fifth Street and visit Something Different Gallery and Horizontal Books for unique gifts and used books.

Something Different Gallery, 1899 W. Twenty-Fifth St.
216-696-5226, somethingdifferentgallery.com

Horizontal Books, 1921 W. Twenty-Fifth St.
216-298-4411
horizontalbooks.com

Honey Hut
4674 State Rd.
216-749-7077
honeyhut.com

Mitchell's Homemade
1867 W. Twenty-Fifth St., Ohio City
216-861-2799
mitchellshomemade.com

Zero Below
1844 Coventry Rd., Cleveland Heights
216-810-6868
facebook.com/ZerBelow

Cooper's Twist & Shake
35766 Lakeshore Blvd., Eastlake
440-946-3376
facebook.com/Coopers-Twist-
Shake-116969905019419

TUCK IN TO
TACO TUESDAY

You don't have to wait until a Tuesday to enjoy an abundance of tacos. Coastal Tacos in the Cleveland Flats overlooks the Cuyahoga River, complete with a large, inviting deck. Go for the fish tacos and tropical hip vibe. For a more ethnic experience, head over to La Plaza Supermarket. Tucked inside the back corner is a small taco stand serving up delicious street tacos. In the Tremont neighborhood, you can't go wrong with Barrio's custom-made tacos that you design yourself. If you can't decide, they offer daily suggestions that are sure to please your taste buds. The Funky Truckeria, owned by two food truck chefs, offers food truck faves and was voted best tacos in the city.

Coastal Taco
1146 Old River Rd.
216-727-0158
coastaltacobar.com

La Plaza Supermarket
13609 Lakewood Heights Blvd.
216-476-8000
facebook.com/La-Plaza-Supermarket-170618169644880

Barrio Tacos
806 Literary Rd., Tremont
216-999-7714
barrio-tacos.com

Funky Truckeria
3200 Greenwich Rd., Norton
330-208-0560
thefunkytruckeria.com

TIP

If you're up for a taco road trip, head west to Sandusky and enjoy the taco creations at OH Taco, located inside the Hotel Kilbourne. You won't be disappointed in the tacos, cocktails, vibe, or harbor views.

OH Taco
223 W. Water St., Sandusky
844-373-2223
oh-taco.com

ORDER A COCKTAIL
WITH A VIEW

Pull up a seat and enjoy some of the best views in the city while sipping on craft cocktails—the city lit up at night while boats make their way along the river. Cleveland offers some of the most memorable views in the Midwest.

Head over to the Cleveland Flats neighborhood and find a spot at Merwin's Wharf. From the patio, edged against the Cuyahoga River's Irishtown Bend, you can enjoy the water and wildlife.

Take things up a notch by literally going up. Take the elevator to the Thirty-Second floor of the Hilton Hotel for an incredible cityscape backdrop.

The best perch for enjoying the sights and sounds of the lake is from Pier W, a cliffside fine dining establishment with one of the best happy hours in the city.

Merwin's Wharf
1785 Merwin Ave.
216-664-5696
clevelandmetroparks.com/parks/
visit/parks/lakefront-reservation/
merwin-s-wharf

Hilton Hotel
100 Lakeside Ave. E.
216-413-5000
hilton.com/en/hotels/ohio/hilton-
cleveland-downtown-CLEDOHH/
index.html

Pier W, 12700 Lake Ave., Lakewood
216-228-2250
pierw.com

FOLLOW THE SWEET TREAT TRAIL

Cleveland has no shortage of places to find unique desserts and treats. Everything from a waffle bar to handcrafted chocolates beckons you to give in to your sweet tooth cravings.

Inside the West Side Market, you'll find Euro Sweets, which offers more than one hundred scrumptious European treats that have all been made locally.

Malley's Chocolates has been creating chocolate confections since 1935 and has grown to include twenty-three stores across the Greater Northeast Ohio region.

Indulge in a decadent delight at the Euro Wafel Bar on the Case Western Reserve Campus. Choose from an array of waffles with toppings from savory to sweet, including chocolate, nutella, fruits, and caramels. You'll find exactly what you need to cure your sweet craving.

Euro Sweets
1979 W. Twenty-Fifth St., Ohio City
216-534-0115
eusweets.com

Malley's Chocolates
13400 Brookpark Rd.
216-325-5570
malleys.com

Euro Wafel Bar
11457 Mayfield Rd.
216-858-9443
eurowafelbar.com

GO GOURMET
BECAUSE DONUTS SHOULD NEVER BE BORING

For those who would like to enjoy a handcrafted pint with their donuts, Brewnuts is just the place. Donuts are made from scratch, with craft beer as their "not so secret" secret ingredient. Unique flavors, such as milk chocolate stout icing with p'nut butter cookie toasted coconut and pb drizzle, keep locals coming back for more. Get there early because once they are gone you'll have to wait until the next day to get your Brewnuts fix.

For the hippy in you, head over to Peace, Love & Little Donuts for donuts that range from groovy (another word for those who like their donuts simple) to funkadelic frosted donuts that come adorned with crazy toppings, such as lemonade, samoas, or cheesecake.

Brewnuts
6501 Detroit Ave.
216-600-9579
brewnutscleveland.com

Peace, Love & Little Donuts
3786 Rocky River Dr., Westpark
216-862-9806
peaceloveandlittledonuts.com

TIP
Donut Fest happens every winter in downtown Cleveland. Local donut shops and restaurants go fryer to fryer to see who can create the tastiest, most unusual donut in the city. Many will enter, but only one will win the much coveted title of "Best Donut."
donutfest.com/cleveland

CAFFEINE ADDICTS UNITE

Coffee lovers will be glad to know that Cleveland is home to numerous independent coffee shops. For those who are always on the hunt for the perfect cuppa joe, this list is a start for you to find your favorite coffee roaster when you visit.

Rising Star Coffee Roasters sources their beans from growers they know, and they know what makes their coffee beans unique. In turn, that coffee is shared with Clevelanders and visitors alike. Lucky us!

Phoenix Coffee has been providing locals their caffeine fix for more than twenty-five years and has five locations strategically placed across the city, so you are never far from your next cup.

The new kid on the coffee block is Duck-Rabbit. They arrived with a no-holds-barred attitude and are charming customers with their beautifully crafted coffee selections.

Rising Star Coffee Roasters
13368 Madison Ave., Lakewood
216-903-6709
risingstarcoffee.com

Phoenix Coffee
1728 St. Clair Ave.
216-522-9744
phoenixcoffee.com

Duck-Rabbit
2135 Columbus Rd.
duckrabbitcoffee.com

GRAB A SLICE
OF THE PIZZA PIE

Pizza in Cleveland may not have the notoriety of New York City's slices or Chicago's deep dish, but its pizza scene is on the rise.

Il Rione is the place to go if you are craving a New York City slice of pie. Pizza made in the open kitchen plus a beer and wine selection give locals and visitors another reason to visit Gordon Square.

Want wood-fired pizza? Head to Masthead Brewing, located in a 1920s building. It is known for serving beer and pizza. You order at the bar and grab a seat at one of the many rows of picnic tables, a la beer hall style.

Vero Pizza Napoletana is a hidden gem among pizza connoisseurs. Located in a small store front on Cleveland's east side, it is winning customers with its true Italian thin crust and mouthwatering toppings.

Il Rione
1303 W. Sixty-Fifth St.
216-282-1451
ilrionepizzeria.com

Masthead Brewing
1261 Superior Ave.
216-206-6176
mastheadbrewingco.com/our-beer

Vero Pizza Napoletana
12421 Cedar Rd., Cleveland Heights
216-229-8383
verocleveland.com

INDULGE
IN AUTHENTIC ITALIAN
IN LITTLE ITALY

Looking for a trendy neighborhood with an old-world neighborhood charm? Look no further than Little Italy. You'll want to leave time to stroll the district, packed with authentic Italian restaurants, art galleries, and boutiques, before or after your meal.

Maxi's in Little Italy has an energetic atmosphere and welcoming vibe. You can enjoy a delicious array of Italian dishes on a charming patio space.

To create Michelangelo's, take one carriage house, remodel to convert it to a warm, cozy setting complete with dark, rich tones, white tablecloth-topped tables, a fireplace, and wine bar. Add one of the top chefs in the city and you end up with one of Clevelanders' favorite places to dine in Little Italy.

Mama Santa's is a hot spot in the Little Italy neighborhood, and when you try their pizza and house-made noodles, you'll know why.

Maxi's in Little Italy	Michelangelo's
12113 Mayfield Rd.	2198 Murray Hill Rd.
216-421-1500	216-721-0300
maxisbistro.com	mangelos.com

Mama Santa's
12301 Mayfield Rd.
216-421-2159
mamasantas.com

SAVOR A SAPPY STORY
WITH A SWEET ENDING AT THE BURTON CABIN

When it comes to maple syrup production, Ohio is a top producer of the sweet goodness that we love to eat on our pancakes. You can find many places around Northeast Ohio to get your syrup fix, but none may be as charming as the Burton Log Cabin. Modeled after the modest log cabin in Kentucky where Abraham Lincoln was born, Burton Log Cabin has been welcoming guests to step inside its log-fire-warmed interior since 1931 to watch craftsmen turn maple sap into amber streams of deliciousness.

Burton Cabin
14590 E. Park St., Burton
440-834-4204
store.burtonchamberofcommerce.org

TOUR GREAT LAKES
BREWING COMPANY,
OHIO'S LARGEST CRAFT BREWERY

The craft brewery scene is heating up, and the Great Lakes Brewing Company seems to be leading the pack as the largest craft brewery in the state of Ohio. Craft beer connoisseurs and those who simply appreciate a great story with their beer will enjoy a trip to the Ohio City complex for a behind-the-scenes tour. For less than the price of a single beer at the bar, guests will get a glimpse into the history of GLBC, which includes bullet holes in the wall from an assassination attempt on former Prohibition agent and Cleveland Safety Director Eliot Ness. Your tour includes a step-by-step look at the beermaking process and four tokens to sample some of their flagship beer.

Great Lakes Brewing Company
2516 Market Ave.
216-771-4404
greatlakesbrewing.com

TIP
Check out the labels on each variety of GLBC beer,
which share the story of the brew and brewery.

SAY CHEERS
TO OHIO WINES AND WINERIES

Ohio has a long history of winemaking. Winemakers began to grow grapes in the 1800s, and business was good until it was crushed by Prohibition. The 1960s brought a renewed interest in wine production, which continues to grow in popularity. Today, Ohio is one of the top wine-producing states, with many places to sit and sip.

A new phenomenon, the CLE Urban Winery is an upscale, chic, and trendy facility in the historic Cedar-Lee district in Cleveland Heights. All wines are bottled on-site and given Cleveland-centric names, such as Rust Belt Rose and Mighty Cuyahoga Merlot, to honor and celebrate the city of Cleveland.

If you're looking for a romantic getaway near Cleveland, look no further than Gervasi Winery in Canton. Ideal for couples, the Tuscan-inspired grounds feature a spring-fed lake, walking paths, a bistro, and a boutique with beautifully appointed villas.

Firelands Winery has been making wine in Sandusky since 1880. They offer tours, tastings, a gift shop, and Osteria Gusto, a new exposition kitchen that allows visitors to watch the chef prepare beautifully plated morsels while guests sip a perfectly paired glass of wine from the wine service bar.

Enjoy a glass of vino in the outdoor pavilion at Vermilion Valley Vineyards. Their wine is produced from sustainable farming practices and bottled on the rural boutique property south of Vermilion.

Debonne Vineyards is the largest estate winery in Ohio, with more than 175 acres of vines. They were the very first Ohio winery to open an on-site brewery. Debonne Vineyards offers a large selection of wines and specializes in *vinifera* and French-American hybrid vines.

CLE Urban Winery
2180B Lee Rd., Cleveland Heights
216-417-8313
cleurbanwinery.com

Firelands Winery
917 Bardshar Rd., Sandusky
419-625-5474
firelandswinery.com

Gervasi Winery
1700 Fifty-Fifth St. NE, Canton
330-497-1000
gervasivineyard.com

Vermilion Valley Vineyards
11005 Gore Orphanage Rd., Wakeman
440-965-5202
vermilion-valleyvineyards.com

Debonne Vineyards
7840 Doty Rd., Madison
440-466-3485
debonne.com

PICK YOUR OWN PRODUCE

Pick-your-own farms offer a variety of fresh fruits and veggies, depending on the season. While there's nothing like the taste of a freshly picked strawberry bursting with flavor, pick-your-own farms offer other benefits that include saving money, getting a bit of exercise outdoors, and seeing where and how your food is grown. Many farms also offer seasonal events and fall festivals with wagon rides. The Cleveland area has many farms that offer pick-your-own services.

Visit Patterson Fruit Farms in June to pick strawberries, and plan a return trip on a fall weekend and hop on a wagon for a ride to the orchards to pick your own apples.

After picking your raspberries at Rosby Greenhouse and Berry Farm, check out the vegetable selections they have available.

Heavenly Hill Farm allows visitors to pick their own apples, pears, and pumpkins, but if you're running short on time, you can also purchase prepicked products.

Patterson Fruit Farms
11411 Caves Rd., Chesterland
440-729-1964
pattersonfarm.com

Rosby Greenhouse and Berry Farm
42 E. Schaaf Rd., Brooklyn Heights
216-661-6102
rosbycompanies.com/berryfarm.htm

Heavenly Hill Farm
18373 State Rd., North Royalton
440-237-8708

MUSIC AND ENTERTAINMENT

BE WOWED
AT WADE OVAL

If it's a Wednesday in summer, that means it's time to grab the lawn chairs, pack a cooler, and make your way to Wade Oval for WOW! Wade Oval Wednesdays, their FREE summer concert series.

Claim a piece of real estate and get ready to enjoy musical stylings from a variety of artists all summer long. Listen to soul, jazz, rockabilly, and everything in between.

Don't have a cooler with you? No worries. Food trucks and food vendors are on hand to dish up some tasty treats. Concerts begin at 6:00 p.m. and end around 9:00 p.m.

Find Wade Oval in the heart of University Circle between the Cleveland Museum of Art and the Cleveland Museum of Natural History. Park at a nearby museum and stroll over to the Oval.

10820 East Blvd.
universitycircle.org/events/2018/06/13/wow-wade-oval-wednesdays

MEET FUZZY, GIANT MONSTERS
AT THE CLEVELAND KURENTOVANJE

Kurentovanje (koo-rahn-toh-VAHN-yay), a Slovenian-style Mardi Gras, is held each winter in the Slovenian neighborhood. During the four-day festival, the streets fill with vendors, activities, food, and music.

Kurentovanje is celebrated in Slovenia to bring together culture, arts, and people from all over Europe. In the United States, you'll only find the festival in Cleveland.

The highlight of the festival is the parade, which features the release of Kurent, a seven-foot-tall abominable snowman–looking creature wearing bells, feathers, and streamers, whose job it is to chase away winter and usher in spring. Besides the Kurent, the parade includes polka and marching bands, dance troupes, and other community groups.

Join in the revelry by dressing as your own unique Kurent!

6417 Saint Clair Ave.
clevelandkurentovanje.com

HAVE A REEL GOOD TIME
AT CLEVELAND CINEMA

As soon as the schedule for the Cleveland International Film Festival is released, those hungry for the chance to see the best international films begin to pour over it. Locals and visitors alike comb through the guide while discussing films, making selections, and setting dates. This is one of THE not-to-miss spring events. Films are carefully reviewed to give moviegoers the best of new and renowned filmmakers from around the world as well as films from local and regional directors.

Didn't make it to the festival? No worries. Cleveland is fortunate to have a couple of cinemas that showcase films you won't see at your typical movie theater.

The Cleveland Cinematheque is located inside the Cleveland Institute of Art and is one of the country's best repertory movie theaters, according to the *New York Times*. It features themed showings of classic, foreign, and independent films fifty weekends of the year.

Indie films and a monthly screening of *The Rocky Horror Picture Show* can be found at the arthouse favorite Cedar Lee Theatre.

Cleveland International Film Festival
230 W. Huron Rd.
216-623-3456
clevelandfilm.org

Cleveland Cinematheque
11610 Euclid Ave.
216-421-7450
cia.edu/cinematheque

Lee Rd., Cleveland Heights
216-321-5411
clevelandcinemas.com/location/6129/Cedar-Lee-
Theatre-Showtimes

SEE ART AND ARCHITECTURE COLLIDE
AT THE CLEVELAND MUSEUM OF MODERN ART

Those passing by the Cleveland Museum of Contemporary Art can't help but be mesmerized by the sleek, mirrored exterior of the four-story building designed by Farshid Moussavi. Appreciation of the building may begin on the exterior, but the interior's ever-changing exhibits are equally impressive. The museum is the only one of its kind in Northeast Ohio. In its fifty-year history, the MOCA has hosted installations by Andy Warhol and Roy Lichtenstein as well as up-and-coming regional artists. It presents traveling exhibits and swaps out the collection on display three times a year, so you'll never have the same experience twice. The museum offers additional events that take art to the people through invited speakers, outdoor concerts, and performers. Step inside the ever-evolving world of modern art at the MOCA.

11400 Euclid Ave.
216-421-8671
mocacleveland.org

TIP
The Cleveland Museum of Contemporary Art offers free admission on the first Saturday of each month.

FIND YOUR JAM
AT MUSIC FESTIVALS

It's incredibly easy to find live music at venues throughout the city on any given weekend, but if you want a full musical experience, attend one of the many annual music festivals or summer concert series.

Ticket and beer sale profits from Great Lakes Burning River Fest provide cleaner water for Ohio. As a bonus, you get to attend one of the biggest music festivals in the area. Two stages, Great Lakes brews, and food trucks make it a weekend to remember.

On Thursday nights, enjoy the Edgewater Live concert series, with concerts, local food trucks, craft beers, and a variety of other recreational activities.

The LakewoodAlive Front Porch Concert Series presents a show every Friday night during the summer. The series features an eclectic mix of genres, from rock and roll and jazz to reggae and swing.

Great Lakes Burning River Fest
1000 Cuyahoga River Rd.
216-635-3200
burningriverfest.org/getting-here

Edgewater Live
6500 Cleveland Memorial Shoreway
clevelandmetroparks.com/parks/
programs-events/edgewater-live

LakewoodAlive Front Porch Concert Series
15425 Detroit Ave.
216-226-8275
lakewoodalive.org/event/frontporchconcertseries

ENJOY A PLAY
AT KARAMU HOUSE

The name Karamu House is Swahili for "place of joyful meeting" and has been a cultural icon since its conception in 1915. As the oldest African American arts and education organization in the United States, the Karamu House continues to carry out its mission to strengthen the community through theatrical performances and art education. A forty-foot-tall mural of actress Ruby Dee, painted by Kent Twitchell, the godfather of street art, brightens the exterior of Karamu House, while the wood-paneled interior is sprinkled with photos that have captured the history and essence of the community since its inception. Notable artists who have emerged from Karamu House include Langston Hughes, Ron O'Neal, Robert Guillaume, and Imani Hakim. The theater offers a host of classes and workshops in addition to a lineup of plays that run each season.

Karamu House
2355 E. Eighty-Ninth St.
216-795-7070
karamuhouse.org

ENJOY THE SOUNDS
OF THE CLEVELAND ORCHESTRA

Severance Hall is known as one of the world's most beautiful concert halls, and it's only fitting that the stately exterior and elaborate Art Deco interior are home to one of the most revered orchestras in the world. Watching a performance of the Cleveland Orchestra should be on every Clevelander's list of must-do experiences. Luckily for us, the orchestra makes this easy with the annual free "Star-Spangled Spectacular" community concert in Public Square, complete with fireworks. Each summer the orchestra moves its home base to Blossom Music Center, where it offers a variety of concerts. Musicians also venture into such communities as Lakewood, Gordon Square, and Slavic Village for the new "at home" neighborhood residency program to perform in unconventional public spaces to spread the love of music.

Severance Hall
11001 Euclid Ave.
216-231-1111
clevelandorchestra.com

TIP
Download this brochure when attending a concert at Severance Hall and arrive early for a self-guided tour. clevelandorchestra.com/globalassets/1617/pdfs/self-guided-tour-severance-hall.pdf

EXPLORE ARTS
IN COLLINWOOD

The historic Waterloo Arts District in Collinwood is an explosion of creativity and the place to be for those who appreciate art. One walk through the bustling district and you'll discover unique galleries, colorful murals adorning the buildings, sculpture gardens and public art, independent restaurants, and indie music emanating from various venues. Be sure to stop in at the Beachland Ballroom, which started the movement to reclaim the community by providing an intimate venue for local artists and small bands to perform.

The best way to experience the Collinwood renaissance is by participating in Walk All Over Waterloo, which is held the first Friday of each month. Simply view the art and learn about the unique businesses that are now thriving in Collinwood, or if you prefer a more hands-on approach to art and welcome the opportunity to hone your skills, you'll find varied workshops and classes available. Learn dyeing techniques, weaving, and how to spin yarn at Praxis Fiber Workshop. Take a class at Ink House, a satellite of Zygote Press, and learn how fine art prints are made. Or get your hands dirty at BRICK Ceramic + Design Studio, where you can mold your own creation, glaze it, and then fire it.

TIP

The Satellite Gallery is also in the vicinity. It's no longer open, but it's worth walking or driving past to see its unique appearance.

Beachland Ballroom
15711 Waterloo Rd.
216-383-1124
beachlandballroom.com

Walk All Over Waterloo
waterlooarts.org/walk-all-over-waterloo

Praxis Fiber Workshop
15301 Waterloo Rd.
216-644-8661
praxisfiberworkshop.com

Zygote Press Ink House
423 E. 156th St.
zygotepress.com

BRICK Ceramic + Design Studio
420 E. 161st St.
216-744-4689
brickceramics.com

DELVE INTO
THE WORLD OF ROCK AND ROLL

Immerse yourself in the world of rock and roll in this nationally renowned museum full of memorabilia that preserves the history of "rock and roll," a term popularized by Cleveland DJ Alan Freed in 1951. Stroll through exhibits packed with instruments played by the artists, lyrics hand-scribbled on everything from napkins to notebooks, gold records, and stage outfits. Six floors of video, films, and artifacts should satisfy the curiosity of most visitors, but for those who crave more, the Rock & Roll Hall of Fame Library and Archives, located a couple of miles down the road, is open to the public and allows you to further explore your love of music or delve into the life of your favorite artist or band.

Rock & Roll Hall of Fame
1100 E. Ninth St.
216-781-7625
rockhall.com

Rock & Roll Hall of Fame Library and Archives
2809 Woodland Ave.
216-515-1956
library.rockhall.com

TIP
Scheduled appointments are REQUIRED for the Library and Archives.

DO A DOUBLE TAKE
AT THE WORLD'S LARGEST
GATHERING OF TWINS

The annual Twins Days Festival held in Twinsburg, about twenty-five miles southeast of Cleveland, is recognized by Guinness World Records as the largest congregation of twins in the world. It's no surprise that this event has received international recognition and welcomes twins from around the globe for a host of events that include a parade, talent show, and competitions with awards for the most and least alike. This entertaining event doesn't discriminate. Although many sets of multiples attend, you're welcome even if you're not a twin. Visit this fun festival that has taken place every year for forty years to mix and mingle and to see for yourself the lengths this small town goes to live up to its name.

Downtown Twinsburg
330-425-3652
twinsdays.org

CELEBRATE FREE COMIC BOOK DAY

Comic book lovers throughout Cleveland know to mark their calendars for the annual Free Comic Book Day celebration at Carol & John's Comic Book Shop. Whether you're just stepping into the realm of comic books or are a seasoned collector, this family-run shop offers friendly, personable service in a well-organized store full of comic books, graphic novels, and action figures. Don your favorite superhero attire or dress up as your favorite comic figure and line up early for the midnight opening of the shop, which distributes thousands of comic books during the celebration. Outside, you'll find photo ops with the other guests, while indoors, local illustrators dole out their own creations. This two-day, family-friendly event welcomes young and old, and each year brings new additions to an already stellar lineup of events.

Carol & John's Comic Book Shop
17462 Lorain Ave.
216-252-0606
cnjcomics.com

TIP
The Friday night opening is generally for adults, while Saturday offers fun for the entire family.

EXPERIENCE WIZBANG!
A CIRCUS LIKE NO OTHER

Locals Danielle and Jason Tilk have taken their oddball sense of humor, placed it on steroids, and created a memorable, one-of-a-kind, knee-slapping fun circus like no other. Dubbed the Wizbang!, the circus, which started out performing for small audiences, has now grown to include bigger theaters. Wizbang! is a pop-up theater that entertains guests with outrageous antics, circus acts, dance, music, cabaret, and nonstop fun. Enjoy jaw-dropping physical feats, incredible balancing acts, live music that includes everything from an electric guitar to a cello, singing, and much hilarity. The one thing to expect during a Wizbang! show is the unexpected. From one act to the next, you never know what will happen, but you know you'll have fun finding out.

Wizbang!
wizbangtheatre.com/about-forte

DO IT CLEVELAND-STYLE
AT THE POLKA MUSIC HALL OF FAME

Bet polka music is the last thing you expected to see on a list of one hundred things to do in Cleveland before you die, but we'd be remiss if we didn't add it. Cleveland is home to the National Cleveland-Style Polka Hall of Fame. American musicians put their twist on polka, whose musical roots lie in Slovenian folk music, to create some of the happiest music on earth. The museum is located in the Collinwood neighborhood, where greats like Frankie Yankovic, Johnny Vadnal, Johnny Pecon, and Eddie Haba lived. It is open four days a week and is free to visit. Accordions, stage outfits, and artifacts and memorabilia from yesterday and today's polka stars grace the museum. An archive library and polka history video collection are also available at the museum.

National Cleveland-Style Polka Hall of Fame
605 E. 222nd St., Euclid
(866) 66-POLKA (667-6558)
clevelandstyle.com

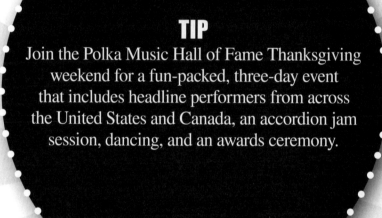

TIP
Join the Polka Music Hall of Fame Thanksgiving weekend for a fun-packed, three-day event that includes headline performers from across the United States and Canada, an accordion jam session, dancing, and an awards ceremony.

ROCK SOME KARAOKE
AT TINA'S NITE CLUB

The nondescript brick building may look a little questionable. There is a reason it has a reputation as a gritty neighborhood dive bar, but it is also known as one of the best karaoke bars in Cleveland. Inside is a low-key bar with scattered tables, brick walls, and basic karaoke equipment. That doesn't stop locals and visitors alike from enjoying the fun atmosphere of Tina's. Since you are in the city that rock and roll built, it only makes sense that you bust out those vocal cords and give it your all. Ask the DJ to load up a classic, such as Joan Jett's "I Love Rock 'n Roll" or Elton John's "Benny and the Jets." Wet your whistle with a shot of your favorite liquor, grab the microphone, and let your inner rock star fly.

Tina's Nite Club
5400 Herman Ave.
facebook.com/pages/Tinas-Nite-Club/216541075035450

TAKE A RIDE TO THE TOP
OF TERMINAL TOWER

Terminal Tower once rose above all other skyscrapers in downtown Cleveland. When it was built in 1930, it was recognized as the tallest building in North America not in New York City and one to be appreciated both inside and out. During the day, the tower is the most recognized building on the Cleveland skyline, and by night it's transformed into a beacon of light that shines across the city. The multicolored LED lights in the tower can be programmed for specific color combinations to show support and awareness of different charities and organizations and celebrate the city's sports teams when they win big. Not for those scared of heights, an observation deck on the forty-second floor opens on the weekends and provides tower visitors a bird's-eye view of the city and thirty miles beyond.

Terminal Tower
230 W. Huron Rd.
216-771-0033
towercitycenter.com

TIP
Call ahead to confirm operating hours before planning your visit to the Observation Deck.

• •

CELEBRATE THE LONGEST DAY OF THE YEAR
AT SUMMER SOLSTICE FESTIVAL

Celebrate the longest day of the year at the annual summer solstice festival hosted by the Cleveland Museum of Art. Enjoy an evening where music and art meld together to bring you a one-of-a-kind event. Headline performers and DJs fly in from around the world to perform on two stages late into the night.

While enjoying cutting-edge sounds, wander around the museum and feast your eyes on the many works of art or take one of the snack-sized guided tours through different galleries.

Plan your visit to Cleveland accordingly and buy Summer Solstice tickets as soon as they go on sale because this is one event that sells out quickly.

11150 East Blvd.
216-421-7350
clevelandart.org

FIND FROZEN FUN
AT NORTH COAST HARBOR ICE FESTIVAL

It's only fitting that an ice festival happens in Cleveland. Cold winters plus a lakefront location make it the perfect event. Ice carvers descend on the city to take massive three-hundred-pound blocks of frozen water and turn them into works of art. Using everything from chainsaws to chisels, the artists take what was once a giant ice cube and leave anything from Superman to a horse head.

After a couple of days of hard work, more than two dozen works of sculpted frozen art, some of it brightly colored and some clear, dot the downtown area between the Rock & Roll Hall of Fame and the Great Lakes Science Center. Ice carving demonstrations, face painting, a fire and ice tower, a scavenger hunt, entertainers, and food trucks all join together for this one-day event. Can't attend? Ice sculptures stay in place until they melt.

North Coast Harbor Ice Festival
northcoastharbor.org/events/event/icefestcle

CATCH A CONCERT
WITH A VIEW AT JACOBS PAVILION

If you like your music with a great view, consider watching your next concert at Jacobs Pavilion. This five-thousand-seat open-air amphitheater is situated in the Flats near the Cuyahoga River and downtown Cleveland and provides an intimate venue for concertgoers. The city skyline makes a breathtaking backdrop for the band as night begins to fall—Tower Terminal and the rest of the city light up and tankers and barges call it a day, pulling in for the night behind the stage. The arena is covered with a pavilion top, so rain or shine, you can relax and enjoy the show as gentle breezes come in off the water.

Jacobs Pavilion
2104 Sycamore St.
nauticaflats.com

GET YOUR ART ON
AT THE MONSTER DRAWING RALLY

The Monster Drawing Rally provides an opportunity for spectators to observe artists in the throes of creative genius. Nearly one hundred local artists participate in this annual fundraising event that takes place at SPACES Gallery. Artwork is created on the spot and immediately put up for grabs for the audience to purchase, with proceeds supporting ongoing exhibitions and residency programs at SPACES.

Families are encouraged to get in on the action by creating their own drawings. The gallery provides materials and displays the drawings on the walls. Who knows? This may be all the encouragement your child needs to jump-start a career in the arts.

SPACES Gallery
2900 Detroit Ave.
216-621-2314
spacesgallery.org

RIDE THE FERRIS WHEEL
AT THE I-X CENTER AMUSEMENT PARK

The I-X Center is the largest convention and exhibition center in Cleveland and the home of several popular events throughout the year. One of the most anticipated events for families may be the annual I-X Indoor Amusement Park, which seems to coincide with spring break. The amusement park is similar to a state fair but held indoors. Games, carnival food, and a variety of rides that appeal to people of all ages entice visitors to visit the event center. While all the rides are fun, the showstopper stands head and shoulders above the rest, literally. The 125-foot Ferris wheel, which protrudes thirty-five feet above the main roof and into a glass atrium, has been a permanent fixture at the I-X Center since it premiered at the 1992 Greater Cleveland Auto Show.

I-X Indoor Amusement Park
One I-X Center Dr.
216-265-2586
ixamusementpark.com/

GET YOUR THRILLS
AT CEDAR POINT

Located almost exactly one hour from downtown Cleveland, Cedar Point Amusement Park provides a fun option for a day or a weekend getaway. The park is known as the Roller Coaster Capital of the World, and this adrenaline junkie's paradise delivers thrills at every twist and turn. With more than seventy rides, including seventeen roller-coasters, this family-friendly park takes fun to new heights. Tamer rides, games, shows, and varied food options are available for those who aren't interested in the thrills or for those who need to catch their breath after a ride on Top Thrill Dragster or Steele Vengeance. All it takes is one visit to realize why thousands of visitors flock to the park in Sandusky each year.

Cedar Point
1 Cedar Point Dr., Sandusky
419-627-2350
cedarpoint.com

TIP
If you can swing it, stay on property at Hotel Breakers for early entry to the park and for access to one of the best beaches along the Lake Erie shoreline.

WATCH A MOVIE
UNDER THE STARS

While drive-in theaters used to be a common sight in many communities, recent years have seen an abandonment of the properties due to rising costs associated with the new digital age. Still, who doesn't have memories of your first drive-in experience? Whether it was watching Disney's *The Rescuers* with extended family or a romantic comedy with the love of your life, the drive-in experience was one that everyone could enjoy. Fortunately, there are several drive-ins in the area that have remained open to ensure that another generation of Clevelanders experiences a double or triple feature movie night under the stars.

TIP
Keep an eye on the weather, as most drive-ins still show movies in rain and fog, and neither provides a great movie-watching experience.

Aut-O-Rama Twin Drive-In
33395 Lorain Rd., North Ridgeville
440-327-9595
autoramadrivein.com

Mayfield Road Drive-In Theater
12100 State Route 322, Chardon
440-286-7173
funflick.com

Magic City Drive-In
5602 S. Cleveland-Massillon Rd., Barberton
330-825-4333
magiccitydrive-in.com

MARVEL AT THE MONUMENTS
IN DOWNTOWN CLEVELAND

The Cuyahoga County Soldiers' and Sailors' Monument may be one of the most recognized landmarks in downtown Cleveland. It is also the starting point for a fun self-guided walking tour that will lead you around the Flats, past Progressive Field, and down Ninth Street, to end right where you started. There are sculptures depicting the likenesses of presidents, athletes, politicians, and other historical figures that were instrumental in the founding of the city. You'll discover memorials that pay homage to public safety workers, such as the Cleveland Fire Fighters Memorial and the Peace Officers Memorial; the Fountain of Eternal Life, a beautiful piece of art; and the quirky *Free Stamp*, a fun, eye-catching (and giant) rubber stamp sculpture by Claes Oldenburg and Coosje van Bruggen that is often seen on Instagram.

Ohio Outdoor Sculpture
oosi.sculpturecenter.org

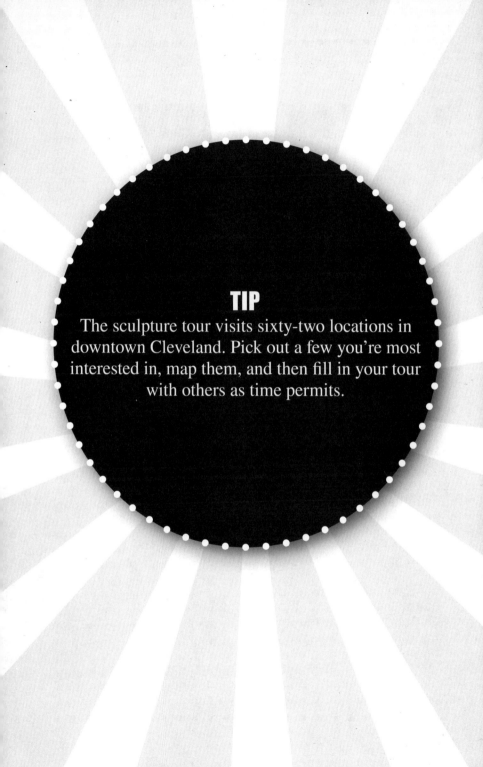

TIP

The sculpture tour visits sixty-two locations in downtown Cleveland. Pick out a few you're most interested in, map them, and then fill in your tour with others as time permits.

KEEP AN EYE OUT FOR ARTISTIC MURALS
IN CLEVELAND

It's amazing what can be done with a can—or fifteen cans—of paint. Artists brighten a drab and dated community and transform it into a vibrant work of art. You'll find that murals are beginning to cover the long-empty walls around the city. Some are fun, some pay homage to people of interest, and some tell a story of the history of the city or political climate of the day. Murals are popping up all over Cleveland, from the Cleveland postcard on one end of Ohio City to Ohio's largest mural on the other, and on many streets in between. Keep your eyes open as you drive through every part of the the city. These pieces of art can be found in many of Cleveland's neighborhoods, such as Ohio City, Waterloo in Collinwood, Gateway, and Tremont.

BLOW YOUR MIND
AT THE GLASS BUBBLE PROJECT

The Glass Bubble Project is heating things up in Ohio City! With a bright abstract mural painted on the side of the building, a door that is normally open, and a pet rooster named Morty, this is one shop that nearly begs you to enter. This artisan studio, located beside the West Side Market, invites visitors to step inside the colorfully painted building for a lesson in glassblowing. Open to all ages, this is a fun stop for a girls' night out, a date with that special someone, or even a day out with the children. The instructors are attentive and patient, ensuring that each participant leaves with a treasured keepsake they can proudly display.

Glass Bubble Project
2421 Bridge Ave.
216-696-7043
glassbubbleproject.com

TIP
It takes a lot of heat to melt glass, so consider scheduling this activity during the winter when it's cold outside.

LEARN HOW TO GET YOUR GROOVE ON
AT GOTTA GROOVE RECORDS

It could be the fascination with all things vintage, the argument that vinyl offers better sound quality than digital, or the deliberate act of pulling an LP off the shelf, removing it from the sleeve, and placing it on the turntable to enjoy the sound that emanates as the needle grazes the disc. Maybe it's a combination of all of those, but one thing is for certain—vinyl records are undergoing a resurgence.

Appropriately located in the Rock and Roll City, Gotta Groove Records opened its Cleveland location in 2009. From a first order of one hundred records to producing a million records a year, one could say business is booming. While black vinyl is still popular, today the process of producing the records becomes an art form, with specialized records in bright colors and color blends. Take a tour of this company to see all the intricate details involved in creating records that are not only beautiful but also sound great because in the end, that's the only thing that matters.

Gotta Groove Records
3615 Superior Ave.
216-431-7373
gottagrooverecords.com

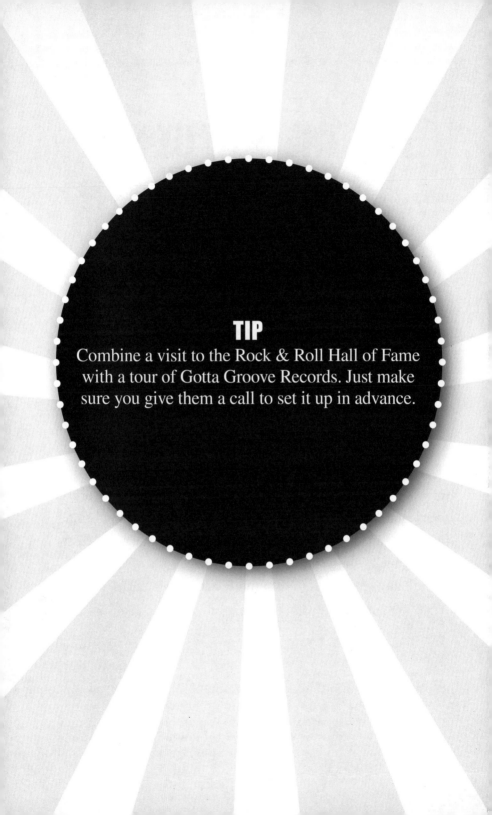

TIP

Combine a visit to the Rock & Roll Hall of Fame with a tour of Gotta Groove Records. Just make sure you give them a call to set it up in advance.

FEEL THE BEAT OF THE WORLD'S LARGEST DRUMSTICKS
IN DAVID GROHL ALLEY

If you're not paying attention, it's easy to miss the one-way alley that runs alongside Burger King in downtown Warren. The passageway has been transformed into a tribute to Dave Grohl. The former drummer for the Rock & Roll Hall of Fame inductee Nirvana now serves as the frontman for the Foo Fighters. He is recognized as a hometown hero, and many say he is the nicest guy in the rock and roll industry. To honor his accomplishments and inspire the youth in the community to work toward achieving their dreams, the alley has been transformed into a shrine for the rock legend. A metal sculpture depicts a likeness of Grohl behind the drums and is surrounded by murals painted by local artists, but the main draw and fun photo op is the set of drumsticks found midway that weigh in at more than nine hundred pounds.

David Grohl Alley
Warren
exploretrumbullcounty.com

ENJOY FREE CONCERTS
AT THE CLEVELAND INSTITUTE OF MUSIC

Indulge in the hushed quiet of the concert hall venue and the incredible sounds at the renowned Cleveland Institute of Music. Many of the concert offerings are open and free to the public, making this an easy concert to say yes to during your visit. It's perfect for orchestral music fans and a great way to introduce children to classical music. You'll hear everything from students practicing or performing recitals to incredibly talented faculty members continuing to share their musical skills. At other times, an ensemble will perform as part of a regular series. Take the time to appreciate the talent of these up-and-coming musical greats while it doesn't cost anything. The next time you hear them they might just be playing as part of the Cleveland Orchestra at Severance Hall.

11021 East Blvd.
216-791-5000
cim.edu

SPORTS AND RECREATION

EXPLORE THE EMERALD NECKLACE

The Cleveland Metroparks are a true jewel to the city. Eighteen reservations currently comprise more than twenty-three thousand acres in and around Cleveland to form the Emerald Necklace. Each park offers its own unique features, from stunning scenery to historic happenings to special in-park attractions.

Rocky River Reservation represents the first land purchased by the park system and sports the Stinchcomb-Groth Memorial Scenic Overlook, where free summer concerts are held.

The Scenic Loop Trail in the North Chagrin Reservation is one of the best places to view spring wildflowers, and the on-site Squire's Castle allows little ones to imagine they are among royalty.

The Ohio & Erie Canal Reservation follows the historic towpath used during Ohio's canal days.

The Chalet in the Mill Stream Run Reservation is home to twin seven-hundred-foot refrigerated toboggan chutes that operate with or without snow.

Stinchcomb-Groth Memorial Scenic Overlook
clevelandmetroparks.com/Main/Stinchcomb-Groth-
Memorial-Scenic-Overlook.aspx

North Chagrin Reservation
3037 Som Center Rd.
440-473-3370
clevelandmetroparks.com/parks/visit/parks/north-
chagrin-reservation

Ohio & Erie Canal Reservation
4150 E. Forty-Ninth St., Cuyahoga Falls
216-206-1000
clevelandmetroparks.com/parks/visit/parks/ohio-erie-
canal-reservation

The Chalet at Mill Stream Run Reservation
16200 Valley Pkwy., Strongsville
440-734-6660
clevelandmetroparks.com/Main/toboggan-chutes.aspx

GET OUT OF DODGE
AND CAMP AT CLAY'S RESORT

Get outside the city and head directly south to Clay's Park Resort for fun, relaxation, and plenty of opportunities to make memories with your family. With more than five hundred acres, this resort includes an adventure waterpark in the 10-acre man-made lake with ziplines, inflatables and water slides for the adventurous and kayaks, canoes, and SUPs for those looking to enjoy the water without necessarily getting wet. An eighteen-hole miniature golf course, heated indoor pool, and twenty-acre fishing lake further demonstrate why families flock to Clay's Park year after year. The family-friendly property is also a popular event venue and has special events throughout the year. Plan a quick weekend getaway or attend one of the many festivals offered throughout the summer season. Enjoy time around the campfire with your family because you've probably heard that families that play together stay together.

Clay's Park Resort
13190 Patterson St. NW, North Lawrence
330-854-6691
clayspark.com

TIP

Purchase your tickets and reserve your campsite as far in advance as possible if you plan to attend an event.

STEP INTO THE WORLD OF THE NFL
AT THE PRO FOOTBALL HALL OF FAME

A visit to the Pro Football Hall of Fame in Canton is a must for anyone who loves the game, but even those who aren't football enthusiasts will enjoy a visit. Learn about the history of football and the founding of the NFL through a series of interactive exhibits—some that you watch, some you touch—that are all filled with artifacts from the game. Memorabilia on display include over three million photos, a collection of the much-coveted Super Bowl rings, and a Bronze Bust Gallery that pays homage to legends of the game. Visitors even have a chance to sit in a themed locker room and watch as the holographic figures of football legends Joe Namath, George Halas, and Vince Lombardi share inspirational lessons learned from football in the *A Game for Life* theater.

Pro Football Hall of Fame
2121 George Halas Dr. NW, Canton
330-456-8207
profootballhof.com

STRAP ON YOUR SKIS
FOR WINTER FUN

Ohio is known for cold, snowy winters, so we may as well make the best of them. Head to Chapin Forest Reservation and strap on your skis or snowshoes to experience cross-country skiing on groomed trails that wind through the countryside.

If you prefer the thrill of downhill skiing, head instead to Boston Mills and Brandywine Ski Resorts in Peninsula. The dual resorts offer a convenient location for someone who wants to hit the slopes after work or for a couple of hours on the weekend. Geared toward beginning and intermediate skiers, this family-friendly resort has trails for all levels, a tubing park, and four terrain parks for snowboarders.

Chapin Forest Reservation
9938 Chillicothe Rd. (Route 306), Kirkland
lakemetroparks.com

Boston Mills and Brandywine Ski Resorts
7100 Riverview Rd., Peninsula
800-875-4241
bnbw.com

TEE IT UP
(OR KICK IT AROUND)
AT CLEVELAND'S MANY GOLF VENUES

Think there is only one way to golf in Cleveland? Think again. Variety is the spice of life, and Clevelanders like their spice hot!

There is the traditional eighteen holes of golf. Tee off at two favorites: Mallard Creek Golf Club, a thirty-six-hole public golf course set on 350 acres, or Red Tail's course, which features fourteen lakes.

Give your throwing arm a workout with disc golf. Try the course at Veterans Memorial Park in Parma.

A rousing round of putt-putt is perfect for families of all ages. Sweeties Golfland has two fun and colorful eighteen-hole courses.

Want something a little different? Take one soccer ball plus one golf course and enter the game of footgolf. Kick a ball from tee to tee and try to sink the ball in a large bucket-like hole. Give your kicks a try at Shawnee Hills Golf Course in Bedford.

Mallard Creek Golf Club
34500 Royalton Rd., Columbia Station
440-748-8231
themallardcreek.com

Veterans Memorial Park
6328 State Rd., Parma
440-885-8144
cityofparma-oh.gov/en-us/
Recreation-Department.aspx

Sweeties Golfland
6770 Brookpark Rd.
216-472-1340
sweetiesgolfland.com/

Shawnee Hills Golf Course
18753 Egbert Rd., Bedford
440-232-7184
clevelandmetroparks.com/golf/
courses/shawnee-hills-golf-course

TIP

Be sure to visit B.A. Sweeties, the largest candy store in the country, after you finish a round of putt-putt golf. There is an old-style soda shop that serves up unique floats and sundaes with its freshly made ice cream. With more than thirty-six flavors of ice cream made on-site and more than two hundred varieties of soda pop, thousands of options are available and will definitely tempt your taste buds.

B.A. Sweeties
6770 Brookpark Rd.
216-739-2244
sweetiescandy.com/store/pc/home.asp

HAVE A SHUFFLING GOOD TIME
IN FOREST CITY

Step into Forest City Shuffleboard to find one of the largest shuffleboard arenas in the city, with two tabletop courts, five indoor courts, and two outdoor courts for your shuffling fun.

Owner Jim Miketo opened his first shuffleboard arena in Marblehead, about an hour away. Luckily for Clevelanders, he invested in an old supermercado building on the fringe of Ohio City, refurbished it into an open, comfortable gaming and dining space, and brought shuffleboard to Cleveland.

The decor is an old-style varsity theme complete with stadium seats, tables made from basketball court hardwood, and an old scoreboard.

Courts are rented by the hour, and each rental comes with a lesson, so no experience is necessary to try your hand at this sliding game.

4506 Lorain Ave.
216-417-5838
forestcityshuffle.com

TIP

Come for the shuffleboard and stay for the food. The kitchen has rotating guest chefs from local restaurants and food trucks, giving guests the opportunity to try something new with each visit. A full bar offers up speciality cocktails as well as local draft and bottled beers.

TAKE ME OUT
TO THE BALL GAME

There is no denying that Clevelanders are sports obsessed. Home to three major league sports teams and a couple of minor league teams, the city always offers a game in play regardless of when you visit.

Quicken Loans Arena, located in the heart of Cleveland, is home to the NBA Cleveland Cavaliers, the AHL Cleveland Monsters, the AFL Cleveland Gladiators, and a number of premium sporting events throughout the year.

Over at FirstEnergy Stadium, along the Lake Erie shore, you can watch the NFL Cleveland Browns and at Progressive Field, also located downtown, the MLB Cleveland Indians.

Baseball fans can tour Progressive Field several times a day from May to August.

Quicken Loans Arena
1 Center Ct.
216-420-2000
theqarena.com/connect/contact-us

FirstEnergy Stadium
100 Alfred Lerner Way
firstenergystadium.com/stadium-info/about-us/

Progressive Field, 2401 Ontario St.
216-420-HITS (4487)
mlb.com/indians/ballpark

TEST YOUR PINBALL AND ARCADE SKILLS

Bring back some of that youthful fun, when your biggest concern was beating the high score at one of these pinball finds in the city.

B Side is located downstairs from the ever-so-famous Grog Shop. At one time, it was a full arcade bar, but it has since downsized to five pinball machines and four vintage arcade games.

Superelectric Pinball Parlor has twenty different games, ranging from a 1966 Subway challenge to the 2018 Iron Maiden. Located in the artsy Gordon Square district, Superelectric is a fun stop on your way to or from the theater or dinner.

You'll find more than forty classic arcade games at 16-Bit Bar & Arcade. If you are sipping a cocktail, you can play for free!

B Side
2785 Euclid Heights Blvd.
Cleveland Heights
216-932-1966
bsideliquorlounge.com

Superelectric Pinball Parlor
6500 Detroit Ave.
419-215-8797
superelectric.tv

16-Bit Bar & Arcade
15012 Detroit Ave., Lakewood
216-563-1115
16-bitbar.com/cleveland

KICK IT OLD SCHOOL
WITH BOCCE BALL
AND DUCKPIN BOWLING

Bocce Ball courts are popping up all around Cleveland. This ancient lawn game has a pretty simple goal: throw a larger ball as near as possible to the small target ball. You can try your skills at Backyard Bocce in the Flats. This family-friendly establishment has three indoor courts and one outdoors.

For adults-only fun, head over to Wild Eagle Saloon, where the good times fly at their ultimate adult playground, which includes an indoor bocce ball court. Go for bocce ball and stay for good grub and live music.

Duckpin bowling, similar to traditional bowling, includes gently throwing a small ball, slightly larger than a softball, down a lane to knock over as many of the ten short, squat pins as possible. Try your skill at the newly opened Hi and Dry in the Tremont neighborhood.

Backyard Bocce
1059 Old River Rd., Ste. 2
216-523-1507
backyardbocceflats.com

Wild Eagle Saloon
921 Huron Rd. E.
216-465-3225
wildeagle.com

Hi and Dry
2221 Professor Ave.
216-566-9463
hianddrycleveland.com

GO ON SAFARI
AT CLEVELAND METROPARKS ZOO

At the Cleveland Metroparks Zoo, you can watch elephants from above, feed a giraffe, ride a train, and visit more than three thousand animals from six hundred species.

Here you can explore the African Savanna, have an Australian Adventure, watch monkeys swing through the trees, discover tigers, bears, and wolves, and so much more.

Be sure to stroll through the RainForest and experience the jungles of Asia, Africa, and the Americas. The two-level rainforest habitat is one of the largest of its kind in the country. Enter the aviary to watch birds in flight over your head, or hang out with sloths and monkeys. Don't miss the twenty-five-foot waterfall!

The zoo is open year-round except January 1 and December 25 and is a short five miles from downtown.

3900 Wildlife Way
216-661-6500
clevelandmetroparks.com/zoo

TAKE IN A BOUT
WITH THE BURNING RIVER ROLLER DERBY LEAGUE

Get your jam on with Cleveland's Roller Derby league. This premier women's flat track league has three travel teams and four home teams. From moms to a systems analyst, players from around the region train and play hard in this competitive sport.

For more than a decade, this elite crew of jammers, blockers, and pivots has been taking the track by storm and owning their bouts.

Make plans to see league teams compete against each other or visiting travel teams at the Euclid Ice Arena. Most bouts are an hour and a half long, begin an hour after the doors open, and play a doubleheader bill. Stay for one game or both and cheer on your favorite players, all of whom have interesting derby names.

Burning River Roller Derby
burningriverderby.com/schedule

TIP

Try your own skating skills across the street at Pla-Mor Roller Rink. The seventeen-thousand-square-foot skating surface gives you plenty of room to find your own derby skating style.

22466 Shore Center Dr., Euclid
216-731-5000
facebook.com/plamorskating

GET ON THE WATER!

For some of the best kayaking, you'll want to head over to Rocky River Reservation inside the Cleveland Metroparks. Launch here and make your way to Lake Erie to enjoy time on both a river and a Great Lake.

The Vermilion-Lorain Water Trail is twenty-seven miles of paddling fun through the Vermilion River and Black River Reservations, including a scenic jaunt along Lake Erie.

Give urban water fun a try and drop a canoe, kayak, or paddleboard in at the North Coast Harbor. Enjoy views of skyscrapers in the background while you navigate the waterway that laps along downtown Cleveland.

For a fun twist on your kayak adventure, head over to Sandusky and let Paddle & Climb outfit you for a day of fun on Sandusky Bay, with Cedar Point amusement park as your backdrop!

TIP

Find gear rentals here:

Rock and Dock: 1020 E. Ninth St.
216-804-1152, rockanddock.com/rentals

West River Paddling Co.: 655 W. River Rd., Vermilion
440-967-5292, westriverkayak.com

Kayak 41 North: 1500 Scenic Park Dr., Lakewood
866-529-2541, kayak41north.com

Rocky River Reservation
24000 Valley Pkwy., North Olmsted
440-734-6660
clevelandmetroparks.com/parks/visit/parks/
rocky-river-reservation

Vermilion-Lorain Water Trail
51211 North Ridge Rd., Vermilion
1-800-LCM-PARK (526-7275)
metroparks.cc/vermilion-lorain-water-trails.php

Paddle & Climb
305 E. Water St., Sandusky
419-502-1044
paddleandclimb.com

TAKE A SPIN
AROUND THE CLEVELAND VELODROME

Did you know that Cleveland is known as Bicycle City? You'll find Clevelanders pedaling all around the city, the lakefront, and neighboring towns. Regardless of the season, you'll see bikers across the area getting their pedal on. We have our favorite bike shops, and we show up en masse for two of the best bike festivals: Cleveland Critical Mass and NEO Cycle Fest.

When bikers are ready to step it up, they head directly to the Cleveland Velodrome, located in the Slavic Village. At the only velodrome complex in the entire state, bikers show off their mad skills on a 166-meter circular track with fifty-degree corners and fifteen-degree embankments on the straights.

Bleachers and infield seating as well as food and drinks are available for spectators.

5033 Broadway Ave.
216-256-4285
clevelandvelodrome.org

CATCH THE BUZZ
ON BUZZARD DAY

As proof that Clevelanders will celebrate anything, I give you Buzzard Day in Hinckley. The day starts with a scrumptious all-you-can-eat pancake breakfast, followed by a different kind of arts and craft show filled with the interesting and unusual. After browsing, head out on the city streets for some good old-fashioned games.

Of course, the reason everyone is gathered together is to go buzzard spotting at Brongers Park. No worries if you don't spot any. A guest buzzard makes a special appearance at the park during the spotting event.

The day winds down with an adorable pet contest. This is a perfect festival to attend if you are traveling with the family pet.

Buzzard Day
1410 Ridge Rd., Hinckley
330-299-9720
hinckleyohchamber.com/buzzard-day/buzzard-day-2018

LET FIDO RUN
AT THESE DOG PARKS

Cleveland is a dog-friendly town, and you'll find that Fido is welcome here. These dog parks give your dog a chance to be a dog and have some dog playtime while visiting the city.

While the Downtown Cleveland Dog Park may be small and mostly gravel, it does come with incredible views of the river. It's located immediately behind the Settlers Landing train station.

Nearby Lakewood Dog Park offers a lot more room for large dogs to run. Just over a half acre of land is open for dogs to run freely off leash and burn off their energy. Ample public parking makes this an easy stop during travel.

Bow Wow Beach Park in Stow is a large park with grassy knolls, a separate area for small dogs, and a three-acre pond with a sandy beach right in the middle. Open seasonally, this park is every water dog's nirvana.

A complete list of dog parks can be found at dogsinthecle. com/dog-friendly-cleveland/dog-parks.

Lakewood Dog Park
1699 Valley Pkwy., Lakewood
216-364-7275

Downtown Cleveland Dog Park
1505 Merwin Ave.

Bow Wow Beach Park
5027 Stow Rd., Stow

OTHER FUN THINGS TO DO WITH FIDO

- **Drink wine**—you, not your dog, but s/he is welcome to join you. Debonne Cellars, the Winery at Wolf Creek, and Thorncreek Winery are a few local wineries that welcome dogs on their patio.

- **Take a hike**. Cuyahoga Valley National Park allows dogs on its hiking trails, giving both of you one hundred-plus miles to explore by foot and paw.

- **Smell the roses**. Holden Arboretum allows leashed dogs to stroll the gardens and trails with you.

- **Dine al fresco.** An increasing number of restaurants and bars have patios that welcome well-behaved dogs to join their humans. Call ahead to your favorite outdoor dining establishment to confirm pet friendliness.

TAKE TO THE TREES
AT HOLDEN ARBORETUM

Head to Holden Arboretum to have a one-of-a-kind treetop adventure. Walk up a wooden boardwalk ramp that takes you twenty-four feet above the earth. Once the boardwalk ends, the grated hanging bridges suspended in the treetops begin.

Three bridges form a *V* and start on the edge of a ravine. When you start your walk, the ground starts to fall farther and farther away until you are standing sixty-five feet above the forest floor. The walk takes you through the trees, where you are suddenly eye to eye with creatures you once looked up at.

For a higher bird's-eye view, head over to the nearby Kalberer Family Emergent Tower, which rises 120 feet and offers a 360-degree view of the surrounding area.

On clear days, visitors can see all the way to Lake Erie.

Holden Arboretum, 9550 Sperry Rd., Kirtland
holdenarb.org

MAKE A SPLASH
IN PUBLIC SQUARE

Are you looking for a place to cool off on a hot summer day? Pack a picnic lunch, bathing suits for the children, and sunscreen, and head off, not to the beach, but downtown to Public Square. The redesigned space offers a new public splash pad where the young, and occasionally the young at heart, can run, skip, and dodge the sprays of water that emerge from the fountain. When you're finished splashing in the water, grab your lunch and hang out on the green space throwing a Frisbee or ball while you enjoy the view of some of Cleveland's most interesting buildings. Summer isn't the only time to visit. Return in winter when the splash pad is transformed into an ice-skating rink. Restrooms are available in Tower City.

Public Square
50 Public Square
clevelandpublicsquare.com

TIP
Visit clevelandpublicsquare.com for a list
of current events near the splash pad.

TAKE WING
ON THE BIRD TRAILS
IN CLEVELAND

Occasions for birding along Lake Erie are plentiful. With nearly four hundred species of birds found along the shoreline, chances that you'll spot something new are in your favor. The Lake Erie Birding Trail offers opportunities to view waterbirds, marsh birds, ducks, gulls, and raptors. The Cleveland Area Loop provides diverse viewing locations that range from the lakefront to Lake View Cemetery to Cuyahoga Valley National Park.

Formerly a disposal facility for dredge spoils, the Cleveland Lakefront Nature Preserve has become an urban birding hot spot a short drive from downtown and is noteworthy due to the number and variety of sparrows that can be seen during the fall.

The combination of beach, dunes, woods, and open water makes Headlands Dunes State Nature Preserve in Mentor a favorite for birdwatchers. Nearly three hundred species, almost three-fourths of the Ohio bird list, have been found here.

Cuyahoga Valley National Park is a large area featuring diverse habitats with viewing opportunities of both migratory and resident birds. Bald eagles and peregrine falcons are both known to nest in the park.

For winter viewing, check out the area around the Eastlake power plant, where birds are often spotted feeding in the open water created from the warm discharge of the plant.

If you're up for a drive, head west past Sandusky to Magee Marsh. This birding hot spot draws thousands of people from around the world to view the spring migration of warblers during the annual Bird Week event.

Cleveland Lakefront
8701 Lakeshore Blvd. NE
216-377-1348
portofcleveland.com

Headland Dunes State
Nature Preserve
9601 Headlands Rd., Mentor
614-265-6561
naturepreserves.ohiodnr.gov

Cuyahoga Valley National Park
330-657-2752
nps.gov/cuva

Magee Marsh
13229 West State Route 2
Oak Harbor
419-898-0960
wildlife.ohiodnr.gov

RELIVE THE 1950s
WITH A VISIT TO GENEVA-ON-THE-LAKE

Fifty miles east of Cleveland is Geneva-on-the-Lake, a kitschy resort town that looks like it got stuck in a time warp in the 1950s, which is part of the appeal. Visitors will find a busy strip packed with nostalgic ice cream stands, putt-putt golf, burger joints, and arcades. This quaint community is one of the top vacation destinations in Ohio and worthy of the tank of gas it will take to get there. Do yourself a favor and grab a footlong Coney dog from Eddie's Grill with french fries drenched in malt vinegar. Top that off with a crème stick from Madsen Donuts, where the donuts are baked fresh every day. If you prefer something a bit more grown up, skip the donut and grab a glass of fruit wine at Old Firehouse Winery instead. The view can't be beat and neither can the wines. Be warned that once you visit Geneva-on-the-Lake, you'll be hooked and won't be able to stay away.

Eddie's Grill
5377 Lake Rd. E.
Geneva-on-the-Lake
440-466-8720
eddiesgrill.com

Madsen Donuts
5426 Lake Rd. E.
Geneva-on-the-Lake
440-466-5884
madsendonuts.com

Old Firehouse Winery
5499 Lake Rd. E., Geneva-on-the-Lake
440-466-9300
oldfirehousewinery.com

ESCAPE TO ISLAND TIME

Just over an hour by car and thirty minutes by ferry, two island getaways await on South Bass and Kelleys Islands. Both islands offer activities for all ages: fishing, boating, kayaking, short hiking trails, wineries, incredible views, and even a few options for waterfront dining. Kelleys Island is known for great birdwatching and is home to the largest easily accessible glacial grooves in the world. Inscription Rock, another landmark is one of Ohio's most significant rock art sites, featuring designs engraved by North American Indians.

South Bass also boasts Put-in-Bay, an energetic downtown with shops and boutiques to explore by day and plenty of nightlife when the sun goes down. Rent a golf cart to roam around on your own or take a lap around the island on the Put-in-Bay Tour Train, which offers hop-on, hop-off service to several of the island's top attractions. Perry's Victory and International Peace Memorial is the world's most massive Doric column and a focal point of the island. A ride to the top of the column provides a view of the surrounding islands and mainland. Several festivals are held throughout the summer and fall, including the annual Put-in-Bay Music Festival, Wine Festival, and Oktoberfest Weekend.

Miller Ferry	Jet Express
5174 E. Water St., Port Clinton	101 W. Shoreline Dr., Sandusky
800-500-2421	800-245-1538
millerferry.com	jet-express.com

WATCH THE PASSING SCENERY
ON THE CUYAHOGA VALLEY
SCENIC RAILROAD

The Cuyahoga Valley National Park is widely recognized as an important resource for spending time outside and learning about the great outdoors. You can explore the area on a leisurely drive or by hiking the many trails, biking along the towpath, or hitching a ride on the train that runs through the park several times a day between Independence and Akron. The Cuyahoga Valley Scenic Railroad offers hop-on, hop-off service, or you can purchase a three-and-a-half-hour round-trip ticket and enjoy the passing scenery as the urban landscape gives way to wetlands, marshes, and forests. If you download the Train Tracker App, you can listen to audio clips of interesting stories of the park's history. Hop off in Peninsula, which has been voted one of Ohio's best small towns, to explore the historic buildings and to grab a burger at Fisher's Cafe & Pub, or jump off the train in Independence to experience the classic grilled cheese at Melt.

Cuyahoga Valley Scenic Railroad
800-468-4070
cvsr.com

TIP

The dome seats are the perfect way to experience the fall foliage in Ohio's only national park.

CAST YOUR LINES

Fishing is a popular pastime in Ohio, and those serious about the sport can fish all year long. While the warm summer months draw the biggest crowds of anglers to the waters of Lake Erie, those who aren't afraid of a bit of cold take to the lake in swarms to bore holes through the frozen lake to ice fish in heated shanties. Fishermen on and off Lake Erie will find a wide array of fish species, but the most prevalent are Lake Erie perch, walleye, bluegill, smallmouth bass, white bass, and catfish. Fishing charters are a great way to experience the lake for those who don't own their own boat and don't want to fish from the shoreline. Cleveland Metroparks provides a chance to fish Ohio's lakes and rivers. Rocky River Reservation is known for steelhead trout that can be up to thirty inches in length, for those who want to reel in the big catch.

Rocky River Reservation
Valley Pkwy., North Olmsted
440-734-6660
clevelandmetroparks.com

GET SAND BETWEEN YOUR TOES
AT AREA BEACHES

Headlands Beach State Park will make you think you've been teleported to the Atlantic Ocean. This mile-long beach is Ohio's longest and offers a sandy shoreline, part of which is groomed for sunbathers and swimmers, while the other half is left in a natural state awash with driftwood. In addition to enjoying the refreshing waters of Lake Erie, visitors can hike through the adjoining Headlands Dunes State Nature Preserve.

Rent a cabana for a day of R&R or join a game of beach volleyball at Edgewater Beach located in Edgewater Park. This beach offers wonderful views of downtown and also provides a launching point for kayaks. The westernmost part of the beach is open for dogs to run and play in the water.

Headlands Beach State Park
9601 Headlands Rd., Mentor
440-466-8400
parks.ohiodnr.gov/headlandsbeach

Edgewater Beach
6500 Cleveland Memorial Shoreway
216-635-3304
clevelandmetroparks.com/parks/visit/parks/
lakefront-reservation/edgewater-beach

CULTURE AND HISTORY

TAKE A PEEK UNDER THE SEA

AT THE GREATER CLEVELAND AQUARIUM

The FirstEnergy Powerhouse was built in 1892 and renovated in 2012 to become the Greater Cleveland Aquarium. To architecture lovers, the features of this building, from the exposed brick walls to the repurposed coal chutes to the towering smokestacks, will be equally as fascinating as the creatures housed inside. Half a million gallons of water contain fish and other creatures found in Ohio's lakes and rivers as well as exotic sea creatures, such as the moon jellyfish and the giant Pacific octopus. A touch pool contains several species of stingrays for little and big hands to gently touch as they swim past. Perhaps the most popular feature of the aquarium is the underwater Shark SeaTube. Certified scuba divers can slip into their wetsuits and into the water for an up-close and personal experience with the sharks and other sea creatures.

Greater Cleveland Aquarium
2000 Sycamore St.
216-862-8803, greaterclevelandaquarium.com

TIP
Hang out at feeding time to see a frenzy of activity.

TAKE A TRIP
OUT OF THIS WORLD
WITH NASA IN NORTHEAST OHIO

NASA operates ten facilities around the country, and Northeast Ohio is fortunate to have two—the Glenn Research Center near Cleveland Hopkins International Airport and the Plum Brook Station in Sandusky. While Plum Brook does not offer tours, Glenn Research Center opens the doors to its research facility once a month from April to October with advance reservations. Each tour covers a different aspect of the campus, from the wind tunnel to the zero gravity research facility. Space enthusiasts of all ages will be fascinated by the out-of-this-world experience waiting for them when they explore the official NASA Glenn Visitor Center, which is located in the Great Lakes Science Center. Learn what it's like to work in space, locate a real moon rock, take your photo in a spacesuit, and catch a glimpse inside the 1973 Skylab 3 Apollo Command Module. A must for those who have their sights set on space travel.

Glenn Research Center
21000 Brookpark Rd.
216-433-4000
nasa.gov/centers/glenn/
home/index.html

Great Lakes Science Center
601 Erieside Ave.
216-694-2000
greatscience.com

LEARN HISTORY AND CULTURE
AT THE CULTURAL GARDENS

Cleveland is a melting pot of many nationalities, some of which are represented in twenty-six gardens that span two miles along Martin Luther King Boulevard from University Circle to the south and I-90 and the lakefront to the north. The land for the gardens was donated by John D. Rockefeller to provide green space in the city and dates back to 1916, with the development of the Shakespeare Garden, which is now known as the British Garden. Each garden portrays cultural highlights from the representative country. Elaborate water fountains, sculptures, and busts of famous composers, authors, scientists, philosophers, and leaders complete each tranquil setting to provide visitors an opportunity to take a stroll through history and learn about the people and events that shaped the twentieth century

Cleveland Cultural Gardens
750 E. Eighty-Eighth St.
216-220-3075
clevelandculturalgardens.org

TIP
Download the Cleveland Historical 2.0 app for a curated historical tour of each garden.

ENJOY LAKE VIEW CEMETERY—
CLEVELAND'S OUTDOOR MUSEUM

Lake View Cemetery has been compared to an outdoor museum, and for good reason. The elaborate grave markers, monuments, and chapels located on the grounds provide some of the most stunning funerary architecture in Ohio. Highlights of the cemetery include the impressive James A. Garfield Memorial, which is the final resting place of the twentieth president of the United States; Wade Memorial Chapel, whose interior was designed by Louis Comfort Tiffany of New York; and the eerie Haserot angel, which looks as though it has black tears streaming down its face. While beautiful in design and nature, the cemetery is an operational graveyard that serves as the final resting place for many notable Clevelanders, including John D. Rockefeller, Alan Freed, and Carl Stokes.

Lake View Cemetery
12316 Euclid Ave.
216-421-2665
lakeviewcemetery.com

TIP
On a clear day, you can see Lake Erie from the top of the James A. Garfield Memorial.

RELIVE MARITIME HISTORY ON THE USS COD
AND STEAMSHIP WILLIAM G. MATHER

Along Lake Erie rest two vessels from yesteryear, both of which had important roles in maritime history. The USS *Cod* is significant as the last World War II submarine in its original condition, which makes it a national landmark. It is the only submarine memorial that has not been modified for access by civilian visitors, which means that visitors will enter the submarine through the original hatches and climb up and down the original ladders to tour the warship to learn how our servicemen lived and worked at sea.

If you want a history lesson into commercial ship life, look no further than the steamship *William G. Mather*. Built in 1915 as the flagship of the Cleveland-Cliffs Steamship Company, this freighter hauled cargo and ore across the Great Lakes. Take a self-guided tour of the 618-foot-long ship. From the cargo holds to the four-story engine room to the captain's quarters, this ship was state of the art when it was constructed. Don't miss your chance to climb to the top deck for a gorgeous panoramic view of downtown Cleveland.

USS *Cod*	*William G. Mather*
1201 N. Marginal Rd.	601 Erieside Ave.
216-566-8770	216-694-2000
usscod.org	greatscience.com

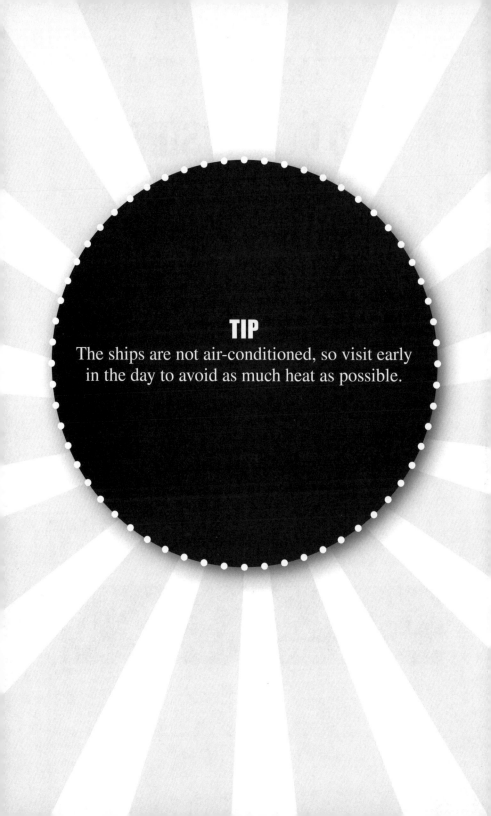

TIP
The ships are not air-conditioned, so visit early in the day to avoid as much heat as possible.

GO DEEP INSIDE
THE WORLD'S LARGEST GEODE

Rock hounds and gem collectors will be astounded to discover that the world's largest geode can be found a short drive and ferry trip away from Cleveland. Located on South Bass Island, Crystal Cave lies beneath the surface of Heineman's Winery, Ohio's oldest family-owned and -operated winery. Tour guides lead thousands of people each year on an adventure forty feet below the surface to share how the cave was discovered when digging a well and how that discovery saved the winery during Prohibition. If you're a fan of all things fun and quirky, it doesn't get much better than a trip inside Crystal Cave.

Crystal Cave
978 Catawba Ave., Put-in-Bay
419-285-2811
heinemanswinery.com/crystalcave.asp

TIP
Enjoy a wine tasting at Heineman's Winery after the tour. Wine is available for adults, while children can enjoy a sample of grape juice.

SPEAK YOUR MIND
AT CITY CLUB

One of the country's most prominent free speech forums resides in Cleveland. Since 1912 the City Club has been welcoming people, from sitting presidents to community activists, to answer questions in a public forum. Continuing in the tradition of creating conversations that help democracy thrive, the club hosts weekly speech forums, which tend to focus on regional and national concerns. Topics are open for discussion on all angles without judgment.

Forums cover topics that include politics, business, social justice, science, arts and culture, public policy, world affairs, and local matters. City Club always hosts forums during the lunch hour on Fridays, but it sponsors a number of other forums throughout the city at different times and locations. You can stumble across a forum at a neighborhood bar, restaurant, museum, or park. Let City Club open your views of the world around you.

City Club
850 Euclid Ave., 2nd Floor
216-621-0082
cityclub.org

STAR LIGHT, STAR BRIGHT,
BE SURE TO VIEW THE STARS TONIGHT

Located on the campus of the Cleveland Museum of Natural History, the Shafran Planetarium and Mueller Observatory take stargazing to a whole new level. The state-of-the-art planetarium introduces guests to the wonders of the night sky around us and takes visitors on a virtual journey beyond our own small universe. As a bonus, during the evening hours, guests can use the building's roof to help find the North Star.

If you're visiting Cleveland from September through May, be sure to visit on a Wednesday when the Mueller Observatory is open to the public. Here you have an excellent vantage point to view the night skies from the historic 10½-inch refracting telescope built by the Warner & Swasey Co. in 1899.

Shafran Planetarium & Mueller Observatory
1 Wade Oval Dr.
216-231-4600
cmnh.org/visit/planetarium-observatory

TAKE AN URBAN HIKE
THROUGH DISTINCTIVE NEIGHBORHOODS

The term "hike" might be a stretch when you take one of these free leisurely walks through one of Cleveland's unique neighborhood districts. Throughout the week, you can join a historic and culture walk through one of six neighborhoods: Gateway District, Warehouse District, Civic Center, Playhouse Square, Canal Basin Park, and University Circle. Guests follow costumed actors or actresses, who portray historical figures and guide you on a ninety-minute walking tour. Learn what makes each neighborhood different and what you absolutely should not miss when visiting each one—from architecture to rivers to the people who made Cleveland what it is today.

Each tour meets in the neighborhood it explores.

Heritage Tourism
clevelandgatewaydistrict.com/history/heritage-tourism

PAY HOMAGE TO SUPERMAN

Fans of one of America's favorite comic book heroes—the one who's faster than a speeding bullet and able to leap tall buildings in a single bound—can visit the homes where inspiration struck and magic happened. Superman was born from Jerry Siegel's imagination, while Joe Shuster brought him to life through his drawings. Together, in 1932, they created one of the most iconic fictional characters of the twentieth century.

Today, Superman aficionados can visit Joe Schuster's house to see where it all began while reading comic strip boards that adorn the fence around the yard. Once you're done paying homage to the birthplace of Superman, visit the historical marker honoring the two men at the northeast corner of East 105th Street and St. Clair Avenue/Highway 283.

10622 Kimberly Ave.

CELEBRATE THE HOLIDAYS AND THE MOVIES— AND HOLIDAY MOVIES—
AT *A CHRISTMAS STORY* HOUSE

Remember the iconic scene of Ralphie shooting his coveted Red Ryder? Walking through that very yard can only happen at *A Christmas Story* House in the Tremont West neighborhood of Cleveland. Ralphie's house really does exist, and luckily for movie lovers everywhere, it is open to the public for tours.

This is the movie set where the kitchen was invaded by turkey-grubbing dogs, where you can climb the staircase that Ralphie walked down in his pink bunny suit, and where you can see the living room where Christmas was unwrapped.

In addition to *A Christmas Story* House, be sure to visit the museum across the street, which is full of memorabilia, props, costumes, hundreds of behind-the-scenes movie photos, and a gift shop.

A Christmas Story House
3159 W. Eleventh St.
achristmasstoryhouse.com

WALK AMONG THE DIVINE
AT THE MUSEUM OF DIVINE STATUES

Holy relics, broken angels, and faded statues have found divine intervention in the form of Lou McClung, local makeup artist and art restorer. Since makeup artistry is second nature to Lou, he quickly became well versed in taking old statues and recasting and fixing them as needed.

Attaching wings, recasting arms, replacing pedestals, and ensuring that the statues are completely intact is the first step. The real magic happens with the second step, when Lou resurrects the lost and forgotten statue with strokes of his paintbrush.

Luckily, visitors can see the restored pieces on display in the Museum of Divine Statues. The museum is dedicated solely to ecclesiastical statues and sacred artifacts of the Catholic church. You can also view relics, chalices, ironwork, baptistery gates, and stained-glass windows here.

12905 Madison Ave., Lakewood
museumofdivinestatues.com

CHEER ON YOUR FAVORITE CATERPILLAR
AT THE WOOLLYBEAR FESTIVAL

In the science world, the woollybear is a fuzzy little caterpillar. In the Vermilion, Ohio, world, it's a reason to throw a really big festival. The Woollybear Festival, which happens every fall, is one of the largest one-day festivals in the entire state. It features a huge parade that lasts almost two hours and includes pets, marching bands with thousands of musicians, radio and TV personalities, vintage cars, floats, a royal court, and so much more.

Unique to this festival is the opportunity to cheer on your favorite woollybear in the Woollybear 500 Race and enjoy or even participate in the Woollybear Animal Look-A-Like Contest.

Of course, the festival brings entertainment, food booths, craft and merchant vendors, and all the woollybear-branded gear you could possibly want.

Woollybear Festival
5495 Liberty Ave., Vermilion
440-967-4477
vermilionchamber.net/festivals/woolybear

OVERNIGHT WITH FRANK

Are you a fan of Frank Lloyd Wright? Maybe interested in great architectural works? If so, we have the perfect overnight experience for you. Step inside the Louis Penfield house, a short twenty-minute drive from Cleveland, for a one-of-a-kind experience. The home was built for Mr. Penfield, who stood at six feet eight inches, so you'll find taller ceilings, slim ribbon windows, and tall doorways.

Tours aren't available at the Penfield home, but it is available for overnight accommodations. You'll be able to immerse yourself in the history of this living architecture home and fully enjoy Mr. Wright's craftsmanship without the ropes, crowds, or eagle-eyed tour guides telling you to not touch a thing. Instead, book a stay and sleep under the roof of an architectural master!

Penfield House
2203 River Rd., Willoughby Hills
440-867-6667
penfieldhouse.com

SEE MIGRATING MONARCHS AND BUTTERFLIES GALORE
AT THE CLEVELAND BOTANICAL GARDEN

Each fall thousands of monarch butterflies touch down in Cleveland on their journey to warmer temperatures in Mexico. While the butterflies are visible throughout the city, those in the know gather in Wendy Park. With direct access to both Lake Erie and the Cuyahoga River, the park is where the monarch butterflies rest for the evening before moving on.

The monarch migration is incredible to view, but if you need a butterfly fix more than once a year, head to the Cleveland Botanical Garden, where you can see butterflies every day. Stroll the themed, seasonal gardens and welcoming playgrounds and enjoy the many events that take place throughout each season. Then make your way to the glasshouse in time for the butterfly release that takes place at 2:00 p.m. each afternoon. It's truly something to see as butterflies take flight, some landing on bystanders.

Wendy Park Monarch Migration
2800 Whiskey Island
216-631-1800

Cleveland Botanical Gardens
Butterfly Release
11030 East Blvd.
216-721-1600
cbgarden.org

VIEW CLEVELAND FROM THE WATER
ON THE *GOODTIME III*

One of the best ways to view the skyline of Cleveland is from the water of Lake Erie. Luckily for us, Cleveland has a boat tour that can make that happen. The four-deck ship *Goodtime III* is the largest excursion ship in Cleveland. This one-thousand-passenger vessel transports guests along the Cuyahoga River before moving out onto Lake Erie for unparalleled views of the city. Aboard the *Goodtime III* is a good way to glimpse the Cleveland West Pierhead Light, which was constructed in 1911 and is the only lighthouse in the city. The outings offer narrated sightseeing tours of the history of Cleveland, making this a great jumping-off point for those visiting Cleveland for the first time. In addition to the sightseeing cruise, dining cruises and special Friday and Saturday evening tours that offer libations are available for ages twenty-one and over.

Goodtime III
825 E. Ninth St. Pier
216-861-5110
goodtimeiii.com

TIP
Grab a seat on the front section of the middle deck for the best views.

DITCH THE CAR
IN FAVOR OF A LOLLY THE TROLLEY TOUR

Do you get nervous driving in city traffic? Leave the driving to the professionals and hop on the iconic red trolley that departs from the Flats for an entertaining one- to two-hour narrated tour. For more than two decades, Lolly the Trolley has provided sightseeing tours. It doesn't matter if you're visiting the city for the first time or the fifth, or even if you're a resident. You'll likely learn a thing or two as a knowledgeable tour guide shows you all that glitters, from the world's largest chandelier in Playhouse Square to the impressive Cleveland Clinic complex that is so large it has its very own ZIP code.

Lolly the Trolley
1101 Winslow Ave.
216-771-4484
lollytrolley.com

TIP
Start with a City Sightseeing tour on your first trip
and then return for a specialty tour.

LIVE THE FARM LIFE IN THE MIDDLE OF THE CITY
AT THE STEARNS HOMESTEAD

A farm in the middle of the city is rare, but that's what you'll find in Parma. The forty-eight-acre Stearns Homestead is the last remaining working farm in the city and now serves to educate the community in best practices in farming that were used fifty to a hundred years ago. Two homes, a Yankee-style barn, and several outbuildings sit on the property. The Stearns Home, built around 1855, is one of the oldest remaining wood homes in Ohio. The Gibbs house, built in 1920, is often open for tours and is full of early-twentieth-century artifacts. Though the history of the homes and buildings may be intriguing, the real draw for many families isn't so much the past that is preserved at this living museum but the animals that live on the farm. Ducks, rabbits, goats, and horses are some of the livestock that visitors can feed on the weekend.

Stearns Homestead, 6975 Ridge Rd., Parma
440-845-9770
stearnshomestead.com

TIP

This is a working farm, so leave your Sunday best in your closet and throw on some comfy clothes that won't be ruined by a bit of dirt.

EXPLORE A CENTURY OF LIGHT
AT THE FAIRPORT HARBOR MARINE MUSEUM AND LIGHTHOUSE

Once known as a prominent shipping port, Fairport Harbor is one of the stops along Lake Erie with a lighthouse. Perched on a hillside, it overlooks the lake near Headlands Beach State Park, voted one of the best beaches in Ohio. The original lighthouse was completed in 1825. Due to deterioration, it had to be rebuilt in 1871, and it operated until 1925, when the Fairport Harbor West Breakwater Lighthouse, which is visible from the original lighthouse, was built. The government wanted to demolish the structure, but it was saved by public outcry. Today, it tells an important piece of Ohio's history as one of the final stops along the Underground Railroad and is the first Great Lakes Lighthouse Museum in the United States. Attached to the lighthouse is the keeper's quarters-turned-museum, which houses Coast Guard uniforms, models of freighters, and other nautical artifacts. Climb the sixty-nine steps to the observation deck for a panoramic view of Lake Erie. Those who seek out all things creepy will be intrigued by the ghost cat that is said to haunt the purr-emises.

Fairport Harbor Marine Museum and Lighthouse
129 Second St., Fairport Harbor
440-354-4825
fairportharborlighthouse.org

TAKE A DAY TRIP
TO AMISH COUNTRY IN GEAUGA COUNTY

Ohio boasts the largest Amish population in the United States, and one of the largest concentrations of Amish in the Buckeye State can be found in Geauga County, a short drive from Cleveland. Start your visit to the community at the Amish-owned and -operated Middlefield Cheese Co-op and Ruthenbuhler Cheese Chalet. Watch cheese being made at the co-op, and then learn the history of Middlefield Cheese. Next, visit the chalet to stock up on deli meats, Middlefield's Swiss cheese, and all the fixins for a picnic before you head out on a country drive along the area's back roads. Get a glimpse of the Amish lifestyle as you pass Amish homes, schools, and horse-drawn carriages and buggies. Continue on Nauvoo Road to find an eclectic mix of shops to explore, from antiques, beads, and jewelry to unique flea market finds and even livestock on auction day.

Middlefield Cheese Co-op
16942 Kinsman Rd., Middlefield
440-632-5567

Rothenbuhler Cheese Chalet
15815 Nauvoo Rd., Middlefield
440-632-6000
rothenbuhlercheesemakers.com

TIP
Amish businesses are closed on Sunday,
so plan to visit during the week or on Saturday.

● ●

TURN THE SPOTLIGHT ON HISTORY
AT THE WESTERN RESERVE HISTORICAL SOCIETY

Once know as the Western Reserve, the northeast corner of Ohio—including Cleveland—has a rich history, which is beautifully preserved and displayed in the *Cleveland Starts Here* exhibit at the Western Reserve Historical Society. Whether you're a visitor or a lifelong resident, this museum is a must-stop for anyone interested in the city's history and all things Cleveland and the surrounding region. Guests are immersed in the stories that have knit the city together over the past 220 years to make residents proud to identify as Clevelanders. Located along University Circle, the complex houses the historic Euclid Beach Carousel, a mansion that highlights Cleveland's burgeoning industrial age, and the Crawford Automobile Museum, where you'll find vehicles that were manufactured right here in Ohio!

Western Reserve Historical Society
10825 East Blvd.
216-721-5722
wrhs.org

TIP

The WRHS is a Blue Star Museum and offers free admission to active duty military personnel and up to five family members (including National Guard and Reserves) from Memorial Day weekend through Labor Day.

STEP BACK IN TIME
IN OHIO'S OLDEST GENERAL STORE

Step across the threshold of Ohio's oldest general store and into the past. The End of the Commons is located forty-five minutes east of Cleveland at the confluence of Geauga, Ashtabula, and Trumbull Counties and is stocked full of treasures from yesteryear. With sloping wood floors that creak under the weight of your feet and rough-hewn beams overhead, this historic structure dates to the mid-1800s and is listed on the National Register of Historic Places. On the shelves, you'll find penny candies, Amish goods, kitchen gadgets, souvenirs, and more than 150 varieties of glass-bottled soda. An on-site café serves simple meals of sandwiches, fries, and ice cream, and a 1940s-themed gas station will keep you fueled up as you explore the countryside.

The End of the Commons General Store
4366 Kinsman Rd., Mesopotamia
440-693-4295
endofthecommons.com

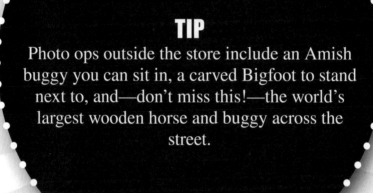

TIP

Photo ops outside the store include an Amish buggy you can sit in, a carved Bigfoot to stand next to, and—don't miss this!—the world's largest wooden horse and buggy across the street.

FIND NATURE IN THE CITY
AT THE ROCKEFELLER PARK GREENHOUSE

The Rockefeller Park Greenhouse may be the best-kept secret in Cleveland. Located by the Cleveland Cultural Gardens, the greenhouse has been in operation for more than a century and is free to visitors. Something is always blooming in the park, which makes this a fun attraction to visit again and again.

Indoors, visitors can enjoy the tranquil sounds of the waterfall surrounded by tropical plants. Outdoors, you'll see a variety of plants along shaded walkways, sculptures representing the four seasons in the courtyard, a Japanese garden, and a gazebo in the Peace Garden.

Escape the bustling city to a quiet haven of green space. On any given day, you're likely to find a shutterbug or two photographing the flora, including a collection of orchids, as well as a young family enjoying a stroll along the grounds.

Rockefeller Park Greenhouse, 750 E. Eighty-Eighth St.
216-664-3103
rockefellergreenhouse.org

SOAR THROUGH FASCINATING HISTORY
AT THE INTERNATIONAL WOMEN'S AIR & SPACE MUSEUM

Tucked away inside the terminal of Burke Lakefront Airport is a little-known museum that honors women who have soared to new heights in the realm of aeronautics. The International Women's Air & Space Museum sheds light on the important role women have played in the history of aviation—some of it out of this world!—from the accomplishments of such well-known women as Amelia Earhart and Sally Ride to the lesser-known endeavors of women who hail from Northeast Ohio. It won't take long to go through the exhibits that share memorabilia and artifacts, but the inspiration you'll find will stick with you for a lifetime.

International Women's Air & Space Museum
1501 N. Marginal Rd.
216-623-1111
iwasm.org

SHOPPING AND FASHION

TAKE HOME A LITTLE BIT OF CLEVELAND
FROM THE 5TH STREET ARCADES

Glass-covered streets conjure up images of Paris and Milan, but what if those very same images could be found in the heart of downtown Cleveland? The city boasts two historic glass-covered indoor streets—the 1898 Colonial Arcade and the 1911 Euclid Arcade. These two structures were combined to create one fabulous downtown entertainment destination that shelters visitors from the elements while retaining an outdoor ambiance.

Inside the 5th Street Arcades, the storefronts are spilling over with local small businesses offering food, retail, and art. Have a food craving? There is a good chance the 5th Street Arcades have a restaurant that can help. Need a souvenir? Cleveland souvenirs abound as do items from local artisans. Be sure to stop in and take home a bit of Cleveland with you.

5th Street Arcades
530 Euclid Ave.
216-583-0500
5thstreetarcades.com

GET YOUR GEAR
AT GEIGER'S

Geiger's has been outfitting Clevelanders since 1932 and is the place to shop for all your outdoor needs. It is known for having the highest-quality and best brands for snowsports, outdoor activities, cycling, footwear, and clothing. Generations of families have been trusting Geiger's to help them enjoy the outdoors more.

Geiger's is located in The Ivory on Euclid, a historic structure originally known as the Truman Building. Built in 1911 by architect Willard Hirsch, it is one of only eight buildings that still stand in Cleveland from that time. Be sure to step next door and visit Grocery Store.

Come for the exceptional clothing and outdoor gear. Stay for the history of the building.

Geiger's
1020 Euclid Ave.
216-755-4500
shopgeigers.com/info/downtown-cleveland

EXPLORE ASIA RIGHT HERE IN CLEVELAND
AT THE NIGHT MARKET

No time to make the flight to Asia to experience a night market? No worries. You only have to travel as far as Cleveland to walk through a traditional Asian night market. On the last Friday of each month during the summer, find your way to Old Chinatown and the intersection of Rockwell Avenue and East Twenty-First Street.

More than two hundred vendors line the streets, comprising a blend of farmers market, makers market, food vendors, and entertainers. The event starts at 5:00 p.m., and things don't wrap up until 11:00 p.m. Come hungry because you will want to have a moving dinner by taste testing your way through the food vendors.

The Night Market Cleveland is free to attend and open to everyone. Plus, it's child, pet, and family friendly.

Night Market Cleveland
E. Twenty-First St. and Rockwell Ave.
nightmarketcle.com

HAVE
—YOU GUESSED IT—
LOADS OF FUN
AT THE BIG FUN TOY STORE

Heralded by locals as the Greatest Toy Store on Earth, this toy store is better than any you've ever entered before.

Stepping inside the door of this store is like stepping into a rich relative's playroom that has been hidden away for years—an interesting blend of pure geekiness and a blast from the past. You'll find one-of-a-kind toys and collectibles from the fifties, sixties, and seventies on the stocked-to-capacity shelves mixed with Cleveland souvenirs, classic candy, and fun and quirky novelties, such as Unicorn bandages and "Grow Your Own Weed," um, for medicinal purposes, right? Okay, maybe it's fake, but it's a fun thought for someone on your shopping list. The Big Fun Toy Store is not just for children. This is one stop that mom and pop and even grandma and grandpa will enjoy.

Big Fun Toy Store
1814 Coventry Rd., Cleveland Heights
bigfunbigfun.com

TASTE THE VERY BEST
AT HEINEN'S GROCERY STORE

Unlike a big-box store, Heinen's serves up class and prides itself on high-quality foods with amazing customer service. You can shop from a comprehensive selection of fresh fruits and juices, organic vegetables, whole foods, and health foods. You'll also find lunch foods and bakery items prepared on-site as a great alternative to the downtown restaurants during the lunch hour.

So, whether you need a shot of your favorite organic fair-trade coffee from one of the talented baristas, plan to grab lunch at the Global Grill, which features recipes inspired from around the world, or need to purchase your groceries for the week, Heinen's has you covered. And if the thought of grocery shopping is too much for you to take in, you can relax in the second-floor lounge area, where you can sip samples of wine from the store's extensive collection for the ultimate tasting experience. Who knew that a visit to the grocery store could be such an enjoyable experience?

Heinen's Grocery Store
900 Euclid Ave.
heinens.com/downtown

DISCOVER ALL THINGS VINTAGE
IN THE LORAIN AVENUE ANTIQUE DISTRICT -

If you think all antique stores are the same, you haven't been to the Lorain Avenue Antique District. Whether you're on the hunt for that one special piece to complete a collection or you're simply in the mood for some rainy day (or not) shopping, you'll find a bevy of retailers, and each offers a varied selection. You'll find the area, which runs from Ohio City through the Gordon Square Arts District, is a mecca for those who love all things vintage. Find fine art, furniture, and housewares at Century Antiques, lighting and architectural salvage items at Nook N Cranny, and anything else you could be seeking at Sweet Lorain's. You'll discover clothing, jewelry, furniture, and kitsch as you meander through the area in search of treasures from yesteryear.

Century Antiques
7410 Lorain Ave.
216-281-9145
centuryantiquescleveland.com

Nook N Cranny
5201 Lorain Ave.
216-281-6665 -
nook-n-cranny.business.site

Sweet Lorain
7105 Lorain Ave.
216-281-1959
sweetlorain.com

SPEND A DAY SHOPPING AND MORE
IN CHAGRIN FALLS

One drive through Chagrin Falls and you'll be smitten by this cute-as-a-button village named for the Chagrin River and the waterfall that are visible from the Main Street Bridge. The downtown area is full of a medley of locally owned independent shops and boutiques that offer something for everyone. Some speculate that Bill Watterson, the creator of *Calvin and Hobbes*, drew inspiration for his cartoon strip from the idyllic setting. Pick up a copy of one of his books in the Fireside Book Shop. The bookstore has served the community for more than fifty years, offering three floors of new and used treasures.

The Chagrin Falls Popcorn Shop serves up candy, popcorn, ice cream, and all kinds of sugary goodness with old-fashioned charm. Slip under the iconic red, white, and blue awning and into the sweet shop that has provided treats to the community since 1949.

With unique home decor items, gifts for weddings and baby showers, clothing, art, and costume jewelry, White Magnolia is your go-to for gifts for anyone and everyone on your list and a shop you'll want to visit over and over to browse the ever-changing inventory.

The Original Dave's Cosmic Subs may have started in Chagrin Falls in the colorfully painted building, but the groovy sandwich shops filled with rock and roll memorabilia are spreading love across the country with each bite of the fresh delicious sub.

Round out your visit with a performance at the Chagrin Valley Little Theatre, one of the oldest community theaters in the nation, which has entertained crowds since the 1930s.

Fireside Book Shop
29 N. Franklin St., Chagrin Falls
440-247-4050
firesidebookshop.com

Chagrin Falls Popcorn Shop
53 N. Main St., Chagrin Falls
440-247-6577
chagrinfallspopcorn.com

White Magnolia
46 N. Main St., Chagrin Falls
440-247-5800
facebook.com/
whitemagnoliaboutique/

The Original Dave's Cosmic Subs
9 River St., Chagrin Falls
440-247-9117
davescosmicsubs.com

Chagrin Valley Little Theatre
40 River St., Chagrin Falls
440-247-8955
cvlt.org

SUGGESTED
ITINERARIES

EXPLORE THE GREAT OUTDOORS

H₂O FUN

TEMPT YOUR TASTE BUDS

WEIRD AND WONDERFUL CLEVELAND

ACTIVITIES
BY SEASON

SPRING

SUMMER

FALL

WINTER

INDEX